The Alchemy of Desire

Fusing Passion with Power in Magical Practice

David Langley

Table of Contents

INTRODUCTION

In the enchanted realms of the human psyche and the esoteric dimensions of existence, the ancient art of alchemy beckons, promising the transformation of base elements into noble substances, of lead into gold. Yet, beyond the literal transmutation of metals lies a deeper, more profound alchemy—a spiritual and psychological journey that seeks to transmute the raw materials of desire and power into the refined elixirs of wisdom and enlightenment.

"The Alchemy of Desire: Fusing Passion with Power in Magical Practice" embarks upon this mystical odyssey, inviting readers to embark upon a transformative quest where desire and power are the prima materia, and magic is the crucible in which they are forged. Rooted in the timeless wisdom of alchemical tradition and infused with modern insights from psychology, spirituality, and occult philosophy, this book serves as a guide for seekers of the hidden mysteries, offering a roadmap for every individuals who dare to tread the path of inner alchemy.

This book seeks to unravel the intricate tapestry woven by desire and power, two potent forces shaping the human experience. Desire, with its fiery intensity and insatiable hunger, drives us to seek fulfillment, pushing us to pursue our dreams and aspirations with unwavering fervor. With its commanding presence and irresistible allure, power empowers us to manifest our desires, wielding influence and authority over our lives and the world around us. Yet, like twin flames dancing in the darkness, desire and power are often entwined in a complex and dynamic relationship, each fueling the other in an endless cycle of longing and attainment.

Drawing upon the rich symbolism of alchemy, we delve into the depths of desire, exploring its multifaceted nature and unraveling its mysteries. From the heart's passionate yearnings to the body's primal urges, desire manifests in myriad forms, shaping our thoughts, emotions, and actions. Through the lens of psychology, mythology, and cultural anthropology, we examine the roots of desire, tracing its origins to the dawn of human consciousness and its evolution through the ages.

Likewise, we venture into the realms of power, exploring its many facets and manifestations in magic and mysticism. From the elemental forces of nature to the archetypal realms of the gods and goddesses, power permeates every aspect of existence, infusing it with vitality and dynamism. Yet, power is a double-edged sword, capable of both creation and destruction, liberation and enslavement. Through the teachings of ancient wisdom traditions and the insights of modern occultism, we seek to understand the nature of power and its role in the magical arts.

As we journey deeper into the alchemical mysteries, we discover the transformative potential inherent in the union of desire and power. Like alchemists of old, we learn to transmute the raw materials of our lives—the leaden weights of our fears and limitations—into the golden treasures of our dreams and aspirations. Through ritual, meditation, and inner exploration, we harness the primal energies of desire and power, forging them into tools for personal and spiritual growth.

"The Alchemy of Desire" is more than just a book—it is a roadmap for the soul's journey, a guide for those who seek to unlock the hidden potentials within themselves and the world around them. It is an invitation to embark upon a quest of self-discovery and transformation, where the fires of desire and the waters of power merge in the crucible of the human heart, giving birth to the alchemical gold of wisdom and enlightenment. So, dear reader, I encourage you to join me on this mystical odyssey as together we explore the mysteries of desire, power, and magic and discover the true alchemy of the soul.

CHAPTER I

Understanding Alchemy

Definition and Origins of Alchemy

Alchemy, steeped in mystery and intrigue, is a multifaceted discipline that defies easy definition. At its core, alchemy is a philosophical and proto-scientific tradition that seeks to explore the hidden workings of the universe and the transformative processes inherent in nature. The origins of alchemy can be tracked back to ancient civilizations which includes Egypt, Mesopotamia, and China, where early practitioners sought to unlock the secrets of creation and immortality. The word "alchemy" itself is derived from the Arabic term "al-kīmiyā," which in turn may have its roots in the ancient Egyptian phrase "khem," meaning "black" or "dark," a reference to the Nile delta's rich black soil. However, the true essence of alchemy transcends linguistic and cultural boundaries, embodying a universal quest for spiritual and material transformation.

One of the defining characteristics of alchemy is its use of symbolism and metaphor to convey deeper truths about the nature of reality. Alchemical texts are replete with cryptic imagery and allegorical narratives, where base metals are transmuted into gold, and the philosopher's stone bestows immortality upon its possessor. These symbols are not merely literal representations but serve as keys to unlocking the mysteries of the human psyche and the cosmos. Alchemy, therefore, can be seen as a form of "spiritual chemistry," where the external transmutation processes mirror the soul's inner journey.

The practice of alchemy encompasses a wide range of pursuits, including metallurgy, medicine, astrology, and spiritual enlightenment. In the early stages of its development, alchemy was closely intertwined with the art of metalworking, as practitioners sought to refine ores and alloys in the quest for gold and other precious metals. Yet, as alchemy evolved over time, it expanded beyond the confines of the laboratory, embracing the realms of philosophy, mysticism, and esoteric spirituality.

One of alchemy's central goals is transmuting base metals into gold, a process known as the "Great Work" or "Magnum Opus." While this goal may seem purely materialistic on the surface, it carries profound symbolic significance. In alchemical symbolism, gold represents material wealth, spiritual enlightenment, and the attainment of spiritual perfection. Therefore, the alchemical transmutation of base metals into gold is understood as a metaphor for transforming the soul from a state of spiritual ignorance and impurity to enlightenment and purity.

Another critical concept in alchemy is the notion of the philosopher's stone, a mythical substance said to have the capacity to transmute base metals into gold and also grant eternal life to its possessor. The philosopher's stone is often equated with the divine spark within each individual, representing the potential for spiritual awakening and self-realization. The quest for the philosopher's stone is thus not merely a search for external riches but a journey of inner alchemy, where the seeker strives to unlock the latent powers of the soul and achieve union with the divine.

In addition to its metallurgical pursuits, alchemy also significantly developed early chemistry and pharmacology. Many alchemical texts contain recipes and instructions for the preparation of medicinal potions, elixirs, and tinctures, based on the belief that the same transformative processes that occur in the laboratory could also occur within the human body. Alchemy, therefore, served as a bridge between the material and spiritual worlds, offering insights into the interconnectedness of all things and the potential for holistic healing and transformation.

In conclusion, alchemy is a rich and multifaceted tradition encompassing philosophy, science, and spirituality. Its origins lie in ancient Egypt, Mesopotamia, and China, where early practitioners sought to unlock the secrets of creation and immortality. Alchemy uses symbolism and metaphor to convey deeper truths about the nature of reality, and its goals include the transmutation of base metals into gold and attaining spiritual enlightenment. While alchemy may have its roots in the distant past, its insights into the interconnectedness of all things and the potential for transformation continue to resonate in the modern world.

The Intersection of Desire and Power

The intersection of desire and power is a complex and multifaceted terrain, where the primal forces that drive human motivation and action converge with the dynamics of influence and control. Desire, with its fiery intensity and insatiable hunger, propels us forward, compelling us to pursue our dreams, ambitions, and passions with unwavering enthusiasm. Whether it be the desire for love, success, wealth, or spiritual fulfillment, the yearnings of the human heart serve as powerful catalysts for action, shaping our thoughts, emotions, and behaviors. Yet, desire alone is not enough to realize our goals; it must be coupled with power—the ability to exert influence and effect change in the world.

In its myriad forms, power is the currency of human interaction, governing relationships, institutions, and societies. It is the ability to shape the course of events, to control resources, and to assert one's will upon others. From political leaders and corporate executives to spiritual gurus and cultural icons, those who wield power hold sway over the hearts and minds of others, shaping the fabric of reality according to their own designs. Yet, power is not merely a tool of domination and control; it is also a force for transformation and liberation, empowering individuals to overcome obstacles, achieve their goals, and realize their fullest potential.

At the intersection of desire and power lies the crucible of human ambition, where the quest for personal fulfillment intersects with the dynamics of social hierarchy and influence. Throughout history, individuals and societies have grappled with the ethical implications of power and its relationship to desire, wrestling with questions of justice, fairness, and the common good. From the ancient

Greek philosophers to contemporary social theorists, thinkers have sought to understand the nature of power and its impact on human behavior, illuminating the tensions between individual freedom and collective responsibility.

In psychology, desire and power are seen as fundamental drivers of human behavior, shaping our perceptions, motivations, and relationships. According to motivational theory, desires arise from the tension between our current and desired states, driving us to take action to bridge the gap between the two. On the other hand, power is seen as the ability to satisfy our desires by exerting control over our environment and influencing the behavior of others. Together, desire and power form the basis of human motivation, guiding our choices and shaping our destinies.

In spirituality and mysticism, desire and power take on deeper symbolic meanings, reflecting the eternal struggle between the ego and the soul. Desire, in this context, is often equated with the ego's cravings for worldly pleasures and attachments, which bind us to the birth's and death's cycle. On the other hand, power is seen as the spiritual energy that flows through all things, empowering us to transcend the limitations of the ego and awaken to our true nature as divine beings. Through meditation, prayer, and selfless service, seekers seek to cultivate spiritual power and purify their desires, aligning themselves with the divine will and attaining union with the Absolute.

In conclusion, the intersection of desire and power is a rich and fertile terrain, where the forces that drive human motivation and action intersect with the dynamics of influence and control. Desire, with its fiery intensity and insatiable hunger, propels us forward, compelling us to pursue our dreams and passions with unwavering fervor. In its myriad forms, power is the currency of human interaction, governing relationships, institutions, and societies. Together, desire and power form the basis of human motivation, shaping our choices and destinies. Whether in psychology, spirituality, or social theory, exploring desire and power offers profound insights into the nature of human existence and the dynamics of personal and collective transformation.

Exploring the Concept of Alchemy in Magical Practice

Alchemy, a term derived from the Arabic word "al- kīmiyā," is a multifaceted concept that has captivated the human imagination for centuries. Originating in ancient Egypt and later flourishing in medieval Europe, alchemy is often associated with the quest to transmute base metals into gold—a pursuit that symbolizes the transformation of the mundane into the sublime. However, alchemy is much more than a mere pursuit of material wealth; it is a profound spiritual and philosophical tradition that encompasses the search for inner enlightenment, spiritual evolution, and the attainment of divine wisdom. In the context of magical practice, alchemy is a powerful metaphor for transforming the self and the universe, offering practitioners a rich tapestry of symbols, archetypes, and practices to explore and integrate into their spiritual journey.

At its core, alchemy is a spiritual discipline that desires to uncover the hidden truths of existence and unlock universe's mysteries. Drawing upon Hermeticism, Gnosticism, and Neoplatonism principles, alchemy posits that a hidden unity and interconnectedness is underlying all of creation—a divine essence permeating every aspect of reality. Through alchemy, practitioners seek to attune themselves to this divine essence and align their consciousness with the higher principles and values that govern the cosmos. By cultivating virtues such as purity, integrity, and harmony, practitioners can awaken to their true nature as divine beings and manifest their divine potential in the world.

Moreover, alchemy is a process of inner transformation—a journey of self-discovery, growth, and evolution that unfolds through a series of stages and phases. One of the central themes of alchemical practice is the concept of transmutation—the idea that individuals can undergo profound shifts in consciousness and identity through inner work, self-reflection, and spiritual practice. This process of transmutation is often depicted symbolically as the journey of the alchemist through the stages of nigredo (blackening), albedo (whitening), and rubedo (reddening), each of which corresponds to a stage of inner purification and refinement. By embracing the challenges and trials of the alchemical journey, practitioners can purify their souls, awaken to their true potential, and embody the divine qualities of love, wisdom, and compassion.

Furthermore, alchemy is a holistic practice that integrates elements of psychology, mysticism, and esotericism into a coherent and comprehensive system of spiritual development. Drawing upon the teachings of Carl Jung, alchemy explores the depths of the human psyche, uncovering the archetypal patterns and symbols that shape our thoughts, emotions, and behaviors. Through practices such as dreamwork, active imagination, and symbolic interpretation, practitioners can delve into the hidden recesses of the unconscious mind and uncover the hidden truths that lie buried within. By integrating the conscious and also unconscious aspects of the self, practitioners can achieve a state of wholeness and unity that transcends the limitations of ego and identity.

Moreover, alchemy is a practice of sacred union—a symbolic marriage of opposites, such as masculine and feminine, light and dark, conscious and unconscious. This process of integration and reconciliation involves embracing the polarities of existence and finding balance and harmony within oneself. By uniting the disparate aspects of the self, practitioners can transcend duality and experience a state of wholeness and unity with the cosmos. Through practices such as ritual, meditation, and energy work, practitioners can cultivate a deep sense of connection to the divine and align themselves with the innate rhythms and cycles of the universe.

In addition, alchemy is a practice of co-creation—a collaboration between the practitioner and the divine forces of the universe to bring about positive change in the world. Through rituals, spells, and invocations, practitioners can channel the energies of the cosmos and manifest their intentions with clarity, purpose, and effectiveness. By aligning their will with the divine will, practitioners can become co-creators of their own destiny and participate in the ongoing cosmic evolution and transformation process.

In conclusion, exploring the concept of alchemy in magical practice offers practitioners a rich and multifaceted framework for spiritual growth and self-discovery. Rooted in ancient wisdom and mystical traditions, alchemy provides a powerful set of tools, symbols, and practices to guide individuals on their journey of inner transformation and awakening. By embracing the principles of alchemy and integrating them into their magical practice, practitioners can unlock the hidden potentials within themselves, awaken to their true nature as divine beings, and co-create a more just, equitable, and compassionate world for all beings.

The Importance of Understanding Desire in Magic

Desire is a potent force that permeates every aspect of human existence, profoundly shaping our thoughts, emotions, and actions. In the context of magic, understanding desire is of paramount importance, as it serves as the fuel that drives our intentions and manifests our will into reality. Whether we desire love, wealth, health, or spiritual enlightenment, our desires are potent catalysts for change, serving as the impetus for our magical workings and the foundation upon which our spells and rituals are built.

One of the key reasons why understanding desire is crucial in magic is because it is the guiding force behind our intentions. In magical practice, intentionality is everything—it is the clarity and focus with which we direct our energy and channel our will toward a specific outcome. By understanding our desires and aligning them with our highest values and aspirations, we can cultivate intentions that are clear, focused, and aligned with the greater good. This ensures that our magical workings are conducted with integrity, purpose, and mindfulness, and that they yield results that are in harmony with our truest selves.

Moreover, understanding desire allows us to harness its transformative power in our magical practice. Desire is not merely a fleeting emotion or passing whim—it is a potent energy that has the capacity to shape our reality and create profound shifts in our lives. By understanding the nature of desire and its underlying motivations, we can learn to work with its energy constructively and empoweringly, rather than allowing it to control us or lead us astray. Through visualization, affirmation, and energy work, we can harness the power of desire to manifest our intentions with greater clarity, precision, and effectiveness, thereby transforming our lives in meaningful and positive ways.

Furthermore, understanding desire enables us to uncover the deeper layers of our subconscious mind and address the underlying patterns and beliefs that may influence our magical workings. Often, our desires are rooted in unconscious fears, traumas, and conditioning that we may not be fully aware of. We may begin to untangle the webs of constraint and resistance that might be preventing us from reaching our greatest potential by bringing these hidden facets of ourselves to light. We can go into the depths of our mind through journaling, meditation, and inner work, revealing the underlying reasons for our desires and turning them into opportunities for empowerment and liberation.

Moreover, understanding desire allows us to cultivate a more profound sense of self-awareness and self-compassion in our magical practice. When we understand our desires and their underlying needs and motivations, we can approach ourselves and our magical workings with greater compassion, acceptance, and non-judgment. Rather than condemning ourselves for our desires or attempting to suppress them, we can embrace them as valuable aspects of our human experience, worthy of exploration and understanding. By cultivating self-awareness and self-compassion, we can develop a more authentic and empowered relationship with ourselves and our magical practice, leading to greater fulfillment, authenticity, and well-being.

In addition, understanding desire helps us to cultivate a sense of ethical responsibility in our magical practice. Desire, like any other energy, has the potential to be used for both constructive and destructive purposes, depending on how it is wielded. By understanding our desires and the potential impact of our actions on ourselves and others, we can ensure that our magical workings are conducted with integrity, compassion, and respect for all beings' free will and autonomy. This ensures that our magical practice is aligned with higher principles and values and contributes to the greater good rather than perpetuating harm or imbalance.

In conclusion, the importance of understanding desire in magic cannot be overstated. Desire is the driving force behind our intentions, the fuel that powers our magical workings, and the catalyst for transformation in our lives. By understanding the nature of desire and its underlying motivations, we can harness its transformative power constructively and empoweringly, aligning our intentions with our highest values and aspirations. Through self- awareness, self-compassion, and ethical responsibility, we can cultivate a more authentic and empowered relationship with ourselves and our magical practice, leading to greater fulfillment, authenticity, and well-being in all areas of our lives.

Setting the Stage for Magical Practice

In the vast and mystical landscape of magical practice, the setting in which one engages in rituals, spells, and other esoteric practices plays a crucial role in shaping the efficacy and potency of the work. Setting the stage for magical practice involves creating a sacred space—a sanctuary where the practitioner can connect with the unseen realms, commune with higher powers, and tap into the deep well of inner wisdom. This sacred space serves as a container for the energies invoked during magical rituals, providing a conducive environment for spiritual transformation and manifestation. From the ancient temples of Egypt and Mesopotamia to the modern-day altars and sanctuaries of contemporary practitioners, the art of setting the stage for magical practice has been a cornerstone of esoteric traditions throughout history.

At the heart of setting the stage for magical practice lies the concept of sacred space—a consecrated area imbued with spiritual energy and intention. Sacred space can take many forms, from a simple meditation corner in one's home to an elaborate ritual chamber adorned with symbols, candles, and sacred objects. The key is to create an environment that is free from distractions as well as conducive to deep inner work. This may involve cleansing the space of negative energies, invoking protective spirits or deities, and imbuing the area with blessings and prayers. By consecrating the space in this way, the practitioner creates a potent container for magical energies to flow and manifest.

Central to the creation of sacred space is the use of ritual and ceremony to mark the beginning and end of magical workings. Rituals serve as symbolic acts that help focus the mind, raise energy, and connect with the divine. They may involve the lighting of candles, the ringing of bells, the chanting of incantations, or the performance of symbolic gestures. By engaging in these rituals, the practitioner enters into a state of heightened awareness and receptivity, opening themselves to the energies of the unseen realms and aligning themselves with the forces of creation.

In addition to rituals, setting the stage for magical practice often involves using sacred objects and symbols to imbue the space with spiritual significance. These may include statues or images of deities, crystals, herbs, and other natural materials, as well as symbols and sigils representing specific intentions or energies. Each object is a focal point for the practitioner's attention, helping to anchor their awareness in the present moment and align their energies with the desired outcome of the magical working. Through carefully selecting and placing these sacred objects, the practitioner creates a symbolic landscape that mirrors the inner realms of consciousness and facilitates the flow of magical energies.

Another important aspect of setting the stage for magical practice is cultivating a receptive and open-minded attitude. Magic is a subtle and mysterious art, and its workings often unfold in ways beyond the rational mind's grasp. By approaching magical practice with humility, curiosity, and a willingness to surrender to the unknown, the practitioner opens themselves to the wisdom of the unseen realms and invites synchronicities and serendipities into their lives. This attitude of openness and receptivity is essential for allowing the energies of magic to flow freely and manifest according to divine will.

In conclusion, setting the stage for magical practice is a foundational aspect of esoteric traditions, providing a sacred container for the transformative energies invoked during rituals and spells. By creating a consecrated space, engaging in rituals and ceremonies, using sacred objects and symbols, and cultivating an open-minded attitude, the practitioner establishes a connection with the unseen realms and aligns themselves with the forces of creation. In this sacred space, the practitioner can tap into the deep well of inner wisdom, commune with higher powers, and manifest their intentions with clarity and intention.

CHAPTER II

The Nature of Desire

Historical and Cultural Perspectives on Desire

Desire, with its profound influence on human thought and behavior, has been a subject of fascination and inquiry across diverse historical and cultural contexts. From the ancient civilizations of Mesopotamia as well as Egypt to the modern societies of the 21st century, the nature and significance of desire have been a central theme in philosophical, religious, and artistic discourse. In exploring historical and cultural perspectives on desire, we encounter a rich tapestry of beliefs, values, and practices that shed light on the human condition and the complexities of our inner lives.

In ancient civilizations like Mesopotamia and Egypt, desire was often connected with the gods and goddesses, who were believed to wield immense power over the affairs of mortals. The ancient Mesopotamians, for example, worshipped Ishtar, the goddess of love and fertility, whose divine presence was said to inspire passion and desire in the hearts of men and women. Similarly, the ancient Egyptians revered Hathor, the goddess of love, music, and beauty, who was depicted as a sensual and voluptuous figure, embodying the pleasures of the flesh. In both cultures, desire was seen as a natural and sacred aspect of human experience, intimately connected with the cycles of nature and the divine forces that governed the universe.

In classical antiquity, the Greek and Roman civilizations further explored the complexities of desire through philosophy, literature, and art. The ancient Greeks, in particular, placed a high value on eros, or romantic love, which they saw as a divine force that could inspire creativity, courage, and self-transcendence. In his Symposium, the philosopher Plato famously described eros as a ladder that leads from physical attraction to the contemplation of beauty itself, ultimately culminating in the pursuit of wisdom and virtue. Likewise, the Roman poet Ovid celebrated the joys and sorrows of love in his Metamorphoses, weaving tales of passion, betrayal, and transformation that continue to resonate with readers to this day. In both cultures, desire was seen as a powerful and often disruptive force that could both uplift and ensnare the human soul, leading to both ecstasy and despair.

In medieval Europe, desire took on new dimensions as Christianity spread across the continent, shaping attitudes towards love, sexuality, and the pursuit of worldly pleasures. The medieval theologian Saint Augustine famously wrestled with the nature of desire in his Confessions, describing his own struggles with lust and temptation before ultimately finding redemption in the love of God. Augustine's teachings on desire and sin would profoundly influence Western thought for centuries to come, shaping Christian societies' moral and ethical frameworks. Yet, alongside the ascetic ideals of Christianity, medieval Europe also saw the emergence of courtly love—a romantic ideal that celebrated the virtues of chivalry, nobility, and devotion. The troubadours of Provence, for example, composed lyrical poems and songs that extolled the joys and sorrows of love, depicting desire as a noble and transformative force that could inspire acts of heroism and sacrifice.

In the modern era, exploring desire has taken on new dimensions as societies have grappled with the challenges of industrialization, urbanization, and globalization. The rise of capitalism, with its emphasis on consumption and materialism, has transformed the landscape of desire, commodifying love, beauty, and sexuality in ways that were unimaginable to previous generations. Likewise, the advent of psychoanalysis, pioneered by Sigmund Freud and others, has offered new insights into the workings of the human psyche, revealing the unconscious drives and impulses that shape our desires and motivations. In literature, art, and popular culture, desire continues to be a central theme, explored in works that range from the romantic novels of Jane Austen to the provocative films of Pedro Almodóvar.

In conclusion, historical and cultural perspectives on desire provide an insight into the complex fabric of the human experience by illuminating the ways in which various societies' beliefs, values, and traditions have shaped and been shaped by desire throughout history. From the ancient civilizations of Mesopotamia as well as Egypt to the modern societies of the 21st century, desire has been a central theme in philosophical, religious, and artistic discourse, reflecting the universal human longing for love, fulfillment, and transcendence. By studying historical and cultural perspectives on desire, we gain a more profound understanding of the complexities of the human condition and the enduring power of the passions that drive us.

Psychological Insights into Desire

Desire, with its intricate web of motivations and emotions, has long been a subject of fascination for psychologists seeking to understand the inner workings of the human mind. Rooted in both biological drives and psychological dynamics, desire is fundamental in shaping our thoughts, behaviors, and relationships. From the pioneering theories of Sigmund Freud to contemporary research in cognitive neuroscience, psychologists have explored the myriad facets of desire, shedding light on its origins, mechanisms, and implications for human behavior.

At the heart of many psychological theories of desire lies the concept of motivation—the drive to satisfy our needs and achieve our goals. According to the influential psychoanalytic theory developed by Sigmund Freud, desire is rooted in the unconscious mind, where it arises from the interplay of instinctual drives, childhood experiences, and social conditioning. Three distinct areas of the human psyche were identified by Freud: the id, ego, and superego, each of which plays a role in shaping our desires and motivations. The id, driven by the pleasure principle, seeks immediate gratification of our primal urges and desires, while the ego and superego act as internal regulators, balancing the id's demands with the constraints of social norms and moral values.

Building on Freud's work, later psychologists have explored the role of cognitive processes in shaping desire, emphasizing the importance of beliefs, expectations, and goals in guiding our behavior. According to cognitive theories of desire, our desires are influenced not only by biological drives but also by our perceptions of the world and ourselves. Albert Bandura's social cognitive theory, for example, posits that desire arises from the interaction between environmental influences, personal factors, and behavioral outcomes. Bandura's concept of self-efficacy—the belief in one's ability to achieve desired outcomes—highlights the role of self-perception in motivating and sustaining behavior, suggesting that our beliefs about our own capabilities shape our desires.

In addition to motivational and cognitive factors, psychologists have explored the emotions' role in shaping desire, highlighting the interplay between desire and affective states such as pleasure, arousal, and craving. According to affective theories of desire, our desires are often driven by pursuing positive emotional experiences and avoiding negative ones. For example, the incentive-sensitization theory proposed by Jaak Panksepp suggests that desire arises from the activation of brain circuits involved in the experience of pleasure and reward. Over time, repeated exposure to rewarding stimuli can lead to sensitization of these circuits, resulting in heightened levels of desire and motivation to seek out pleasurable experiences.

In recent years, advances in cognitive neuroscience have provided novel insights into the neural mechanisms underlying desire, revealing the intricate interplay between brain regions involved in reward processing, decision-making, and self-control. Using techniques like functional magnetic resonance imaging (or fMRI) and positron emission tomography (PET), researchers have identified specific brain circuits involved in the experience of desire, including the mesolimbic dopamine system, the prefrontal cortex, and the insula. These findings suggest that desire is not simply a product of conscious thought or deliberation but is rooted in the complex interplay of neural processes that govern our perceptions, emotions, and behaviors.

In conclusion, psychological insights into desire offer a multifaceted understanding of the inner workings of the human mind, illuminating the complex interplay of motivational, cognitive, and emotional processes that shape our desires and motivations. From Freudian psychoanalysis to contemporary cognitive neuroscience, psychologists have explored desire's origins, mechanisms, and implications, shedding light on its role in shaping human behavior and experience. By studying the psychological underpinnings of desire, we gain a more profound comprehension of the factors that drive our thoughts, actions, and relationships, and insights into how we can harness the power of desire to achieve our goals and aspirations.

The Alchemical Symbolism of Desire's Fire

In the mystical tradition of alchemy, desire is often represented by the symbol of fire—a potent and transformative force that consumes, purifies, and transmutes the raw materials of the soul. With its radiant energy and primal intensity, fire serves as a metaphor for the passionate yearnings of the human heart, igniting the flames of longing and aspiration that propel us forward on our spiritual journey. Yet, the symbolism of desire's fire goes beyond mere metaphor, reflecting deeper truths about the nature of desire and its role in the alchemical process of inner transformation.

At its core, desire's fire represents the alchemical process of transmutation—the transformation of base elements into noble substances, of lead into gold. In alchemical symbolism, desire's fire is the crucible in which the raw materials of the soul are heated, melted, and refined, undergoing a process of purification and sublimation that leads to spiritual enlightenment and liberation. Like the alchemical furnace, desire's fire burns away the impurities and limitations that bind us to the material world, allowing the latent potentials of the soul to emerge and flourish.

Desire's fire is also associated with the element of fire in alchemy, which represents the transformative power of the will and the spirit. With its dynamic energy and creative force, fire is seen as the catalyst for change and growth, inspiring us to transcend our limitations and strive for higher states of consciousness. In the alchemical tradition, fire is often depicted as the agent of transformation, the fiery furnace in which the alchemist heats and purifies the prima materia—the raw material of the soul—until it is transmuted into the philosopher's stone, the symbol of spiritual enlightenment and immortality.

Furthermore, desire's fire is linked to the alchemical concept of nigredo, or the blackening stage, which represents the initial phase of the alchemical process where the prima materia is dissolved and broken down. In the symbolism of nigredo, desire's fire serves as the purifying agent that burns away the ego and the illusions of the false self, leaving behind the ashes of the old self to be reborn anew. This process of dissolution and rebirth is essential for spiritual growth and transformation, as it permits us to release the attachments and identifications that keep us bound to the material world and open ourselves to the higher truths of the spiritual realm.

In addition to its transformative power, desire's fire is also associated with the concept of passion—the intense emotional and creative energy that drives us to pursue our dreams as well as aspirations with unwavering fervor. In alchemical symbolism, passion is seen as the fuel that feeds the flames of desire, propelling us forward on our quest for spiritual enlightenment and self-realization. Yet, like fire, passion can be both a blessing and a curse, capable of illuminating the path to enlightenment and consuming us in its fiery embrace. Thus, the alchemist must learn to harness the power of desire's fire wisely, channeling its energies toward the pursuit of higher ideals and spiritual truths.

In conclusion, the alchemical symbolism of desire's fire offers profound insights into the nature of desire and its role in the process of inner transformation. As the fiery crucible in which the raw materials of the soul are purified and transmuted, desire's fire represents the transformative power of passion, creativity, and spiritual aspiration. By embracing the symbolism of desire's fire, the alchemist learns to harness the primal energies of the soul, using them to fuel the fires of spiritual growth and enlightenment. Through the alchemical process of dissolution and rebirth, desire's fire catalyzes profound inner change, leading the seeker on a journey of self-discovery and self-realization.

Desire as a Catalyst for Transformation

Desire, often regarded as a primal and potent force within the human psyche, has long been recognized as a catalyst for transformation in various spiritual and philosophical traditions. From ancient wisdom teachings to modern psychology, the concept of desire has been explored and dissected, revealing its profound influence on human behavior, growth, and evolution. In personal and spiritual development, desire catalyzes transformation—a driving force that propels individuals toward growth, change, and self-realization.

One of the key ways in which desire acts as a catalyst for transformation is by acting as a source of motivation and inspiration. When individuals feel a strong desire for something—a goal, aspiration, or dream—they are often willing to go to great lengths to achieve it. This desire is a powerful motivator, spurring individuals into action and fueling their personal and spiritual growth efforts. Whether it is the desire for love, success, or spiritual enlightenment, the intensity of one's desire can be a driving force that propels them toward their goals and aspirations, catalyzing profound shifts in their lives.

Moreover, desire serves as a catalyst for transformation by acting as a mirror that reflects their deepest longings, fears, and aspirations to individuals. The objects of our desire—the things we crave, yearn for, and fantasize about—often reveal important insights into our true selves and our deepest desires. By examining our desires with curiosity and self-awareness, we can uncover the underlying motivations and needs driving them, gaining valuable insights into our own psychology and the areas of our lives that require healing, growth, or transformation. Through self-reflection and self-inquiry, individuals can gain greater clarity and understanding of themselves, leading to profound shifts in consciousness and behavior.

Furthermore, desire acts as a catalyst for transformation by challenging individuals to step outside of their comfort zones and confront their fears as well as limitations. Pursuing desire often involves taking risks, facing uncertainty, and embracing the unknown—all of which can be uncomfortable and frightening experiences. However, individuals often experience the greatest growth and transformation through these challenges and obstacles. By pushing themselves beyond their perceived limits and venturing into uncharted territory, individuals can expand their horizons, discover new strengths and abilities, and unlock hidden potentials within themselves, leading to profound shifts in consciousness and self-awareness.

In addition, desire catalyzes transformation by igniting the creative spark within individuals and inspiring them to explore new possibilities and potentials. When individuals feel a strong desire for something, whether it is a creative endeavor, a spiritual practice, or a personal goal, they are often motivated to tap into their creative energies and express themselves in new and innovative ways. This creative expression is an outlet for self-discovery, self-expression, and self-realization, allowing individuals to explore their innermost thoughts, feelings, and desires in a safe and supportive environment. Through creative expression, individuals can unleash their imaginations, break free from limiting beliefs, and also tap into the infinite wellspring of inspiration that lies within, leading to profound shifts in consciousness and creativity.

Moreover, desire catalyzes transformation by fostering a sense of purpose and meaning in individuals' lives. When individuals feel a strong desire for something—a sense of calling, mission, or purpose—they are often motivated to align their actions and intentions with their deepest values and aspirations. This sense of purpose serves as a guiding star, guiding individuals on their journey of personal and spiritual growth and providing them with a sense of direction and clarity amidst life's uncertainties. By following their desires and pursuing their passions with courage and conviction, individuals can cultivate a more profound sense of fulfillment, authenticity, and well-being in their lives, leading to profound shifts in consciousness and happiness.

In conclusion, desire is a potent catalyst for transformation in individuals' lives, propelling them towards growth, change, and self-realization. Whether through motivation, self-reflection, creative expression, or a sense of purpose, desire inspires individuals to explore new possibilities, confront their fears, and unlock hidden potentials within themselves. By embracing their desires with curiosity, courage, and self-awareness, individuals can harness the transformative power of desire to cultivate greater fulfillment, authenticity, and well-being in their lives, leading to profound shifts in consciousness and self-awareness.

The Role of Desire in Magical Workings

Desire plays a central and multifaceted role in magical workings, serving as the driving force behind intention, manifestation, and transformation. In magical practice, desire is not merely a fleeting emotion or passing whim but a potent energy that fuels the practitioner's intentions and shapes the outcomes of their rituals, spells, and ceremonies. Whether one desires love, prosperity, healing, or spiritual enlightenment, the intensity and clarity of one's desire are critical factors in the effectiveness and success of their magical workings.

At its core, desire is the fuel that propels intentions into manifestation in magical practice. Intentions are the conscious thoughts, wishes, and goals that practitioners seek to manifest through their magical workings. However, it is desire that imbues these intentions with energy and momentum, propelling them forward towards manifestation. The stronger and more focused the desire, the greater the energy and momentum behind the intention, making it more probable to manifest in the physical realm. Thus, desire acts as a powerful catalyst for bringing one's intentions into reality, shaping the outcomes of their magical workings and influencing the course of their lives.

Moreover, desire serves as a key component of the manifestation process in magical practice. Manifestation is the process of bringing one's desires and intentions into physical form, turning abstract thoughts and ideas into tangible reality. In order for manifestation to occur, practitioners must cultivate a deep sense of desire for the desired outcome, aligning their thoughts, emotions, and actions to bring it into fruition. Through practices such as visualization, affirmation, and energy work, practitioners can harness the power of desire to amplify the energy behind their intentions and accelerate the manifestation process, bringing their desires into reality with greater speed and effectiveness.

Furthermore, desire serves as a catalyst for transformation in magical practice, facilitating profound shifts in consciousness, perception, and behavior. When practitioners desire change or transformation in their lives, they are often motivated to engage in magical workings that align with their intentions, such as rituals, spells, and meditations. Through these practices, practitioners can tap into the transformative power of desire to break free from limiting beliefs, overcome obstacles, and unlock hidden potentials within themselves. By harnessing the energy of desire in their magical workings, practitioners can catalyze personal and spiritual growth, leading to profound shifts in consciousness and self-awareness.

In addition, desire is a source of inspiration and creativity in magical practice, fueling the practitioner's imagination and empowering them to explore new possibilities and potentials. When practitioners strongly desire something—a creative project, a spiritual goal, or a personal aspiration—they are often motivated to tap into their creative energies and express themselves in new and innovative ways. Through practices such as ritual crafting, spellcasting, and energy manipulation, practitioners can channel the energy of desire into their magical workings, infusing them with passion, purpose, and creativity. By harnessing the creative power of desire, practitioners can unlock their creative potential and manifest their desires in unique and imaginative ways, leading to profound shifts in consciousness and expression.

Moreover, desire serves as a bridge between the conscious and subconscious mind in magical practice, facilitating communication and collaboration between the two. The subconscious mind is the repository of our deepest desires, fears, and beliefs, influencing our thoughts, emotions, and behaviors in subtle and often unseen ways. By tapping into the power of desire, practitioners can access the wisdom as well as guidance of the subconscious mind, gaining insights into the underlying motivations and needs driving their magical workings. Through practices such as dreamwork, meditation, and trance induction, practitioners can explore the depths of their subconscious mind, uncovering hidden truths and unlocking the secrets of their innermost selves. By harnessing the power of desire to connect with the subconscious mind, practitioners can deepen their understanding of themselves and their magical practice, leading to profound shifts in consciousness and self-awareness.

In conclusion, desire plays a central and multifaceted role in magical workings, driving intention, manifestation, and transformation. Whether one desires love, prosperity, healing, or spiritual enlightenment, the intensity and clarity of one's desire are critical factors in the effectiveness and success of their magical practice. By harnessing the power of desire in their magical workings, practitioners can amplify the energy behind their intentions, accelerate the manifestation process, catalyze personal and spiritual growth, unlock their creative potential, and deepen their understanding of themselves and their magical practice. Thus, desire is a potent and indispensable tool for practitioners seeking to manifest their desires and transform their lives through magic.

CHAPTER III

The Dynamics of Power

Types and Sources of Magical Power

In magic and mysticism, power is the lifeblood that animates spells, rituals, and other mystical practices, empowering practitioners to manifest their intentions and shape the fabric of reality. Yet, power is not a monolithic force but a complex and multifaceted phenomenon, with various types and sources contributing to its potency and efficacy. Understanding the different types and sources of magical power is essential for practitioners seeking to deepen their knowledge and mastery of the mystical arts, as it allows them to harness and channel these energies by their intentions and goals.

Personal power is one of the primary types of magical power—the innate energy and potential that resides within each individual. Personal power is the result of the unique combination of genetics, upbringing, and life experiences that shape a person's personality, abilities, and talents. Some individuals may have a natural affinity for certain magical practices, while others may need to cultivate their abilities through study, practice, and self- discovery. Personal power can be enhanced through various means, such as meditation, visualization, energy work, and other spiritual practices, allowing practitioners to tap into their inner resources and unleash their full magical potential.

Another type of magical power is elemental power—the energy associated with the four classical elements of earth, air, fire, and water. In many magical traditions, each element is seen as a source of magical energy with its own unique qualities and attributes. Earth, for example, is associated with stability, grounding, and abundance, while air is associated with communication, intellect, and freedom. Fire represents passion, transformation, and purification, while water represents emotions, intuition, and healing. By working with the elemental energies, practitioners can draw upon the strengths of each element to enhance their magical workings and achieve their goals.

Divine power is another critical source of magical energy, deriving from the gods, goddesses, and other divine beings that populate the pantheons of various religious and spiritual traditions. In many cultures, deities are seen as sources of wisdom, guidance, and inspiration, and their blessings are sought by practitioners seeking assistance in their magical endeavors. Whether through prayer, invocation, or ritual offerings, practitioners can invoke the aid of the divine to amplify their magical power and align themselves with higher forces of creation and manifestation. Divine power is often seen as both transcendent and immanent, existing both beyond and within the practitioner, and can be accessed through a deep connection with the divine realms.

In addition to personal, elemental, and divine power, magical practitioners may also draw upon the power of symbols, sigils, and other magical tools to enhance their spells and rituals. Symbols have been used for centuries as vehicles for conveying meaning and intention, and their use in magic is no exception. By imbuing symbols with personal or universal significance, practitioners can tap into their symbolic power to amplify the energies of their magical workings and manifest their desires more effectively. Sigils, particularly, are highly potent symbols created by combining and rearranging letters, numbers, or other symbols to represent specific intentions or desires. When charged with energy and activated through ritual, sigils can serve as powerful conduits for magical power, allowing practitioners to manifest their intentions with precision and efficacy.

In conclusion, the types and sources of magical power are as diverse and multifaceted as the practitioners who seek to harness them. From personal power to elemental energy and divine blessings to symbolic sigils, the sources of magical power offer a wealth of possibilities for those who seek to deepen their understanding and mastery of the mystical arts. By recognizing and working with these sources of power, practitioners can enhance the potency and effectiveness of their magical workings, allowing them to manifest their intentions and achieve their goals with clarity and confidence. Whether drawing upon the energies of the elements, invoking the aid of the divine, or crafting powerful symbols and sigils, the practitioner's ability to tap into the sources of magical power is limited only by their imagination and intention.

Ethics and Responsibility in Power Dynamics

The dynamics of power, with its capacity to influence, control, and shape the lives of individuals and societies, inevitably raise profound ethical questions about the responsible utilization of power and the consequences of its wielders' actions. Whether in personal relationships, professional settings, or broader societal contexts, the ethical considerations surrounding power dynamics are complex and multifaceted, touching upon issues of justice, fairness, accountability, and the common good. In exploring ethics and responsibility in power dynamics, we encounter a rich tapestry of philosophical, psychological, and social perspectives that shed light on the complexities of power and its impact on human behavior and society.

At the heart of ethical considerations in power dynamics lies in how power is acquired, maintained, and exercised. Power is often obtained through legitimate means, such as democratic elections, meritocratic systems, or voluntary agreements between individuals. Yet, power can also be acquired through coercion, manipulation, or exploitation, raising questions about the moral legitimacy of its wielders and the fairness of the systems that grant them authority. Ethical theories including utilitarianism, deontology, and virtue ethics offer different perspectives on the moral dimensions of power, with some emphasizing the importance of maximizing overall happiness or minimizing harm, while others focus on principles of duty, justice, and integrity.

Responsibility in power dynamics extends beyond the mere acquisition and exercise of power to encompass the broader impact of power on individuals and communities. Those who hold positions of power—whether in government, business, or other institutions—have a moral obligation to use their influence in ways that promote the well-being and dignity of others. This entails protecting the rights and interests of marginalized and vulnerable populations, ensuring equitable access to resources and opportunities, and fostering conditions of justice, equality, and human flourishing. Responsibility in power dynamics also entails accountability for one's actions and decisions, including transparency, honesty, and the willingness to accept feedback and criticism from others.

Ethical considerations in power dynamics also extend to interpersonal relationships, where power imbalances can manifest subtly and nuancedly. In intimate partnerships, friendships, and professional collaborations, the dynamics of power can shape the dynamics of trust, communication, and mutual respect. Ethical principles such as autonomy, consent, and reciprocity are essential for ensuring that power dynamics in relationships are healthy, respectful, and consensual. This includes respecting the boundaries and autonomy of others, seeking informed consent in all interactions, and actively working to create conditions of equality and empowerment.

Furthermore, the ethical dimensions of power dynamics are closely intertwined with issues of social justice and systemic oppression. Power structures such as racism, sexism, homophobia, and classism perpetuate inequalities and injustices that undermine the dignity and well-being of marginalized communities. Ethical action in power dynamics requires not only individual integrity and accountability but also collective efforts to challenge and transform unjust systems and institutions. This entails advocating for policies and practices that promote equity and inclusion, amplifying the voices of marginalized groups, and working to dismantle systems of oppression at their roots.

In conclusion, ethics and responsibility in power dynamics are essential considerations for individuals and societies seeking to navigate the complexities of power in a morally responsible manner. Whether in personal relationships, professional settings, or broader societal contexts, the responsible use of power requires integrity, empathy, and a commitment to justice and equity. By upholding ethical principles such as autonomy, consent, and accountability, individuals can foster healthy and respectful power dynamics that honor the dignity and rights of all. Likewise, by challenging systemic injustices and advocating for social change, communities can work towards creating a more just and equitable world where power is wielded responsibly and ethically for the benefit of all.

Unveiling Hidden Power: Accessing and Channeling Energy

Within the realm of magical practice, the concept of energy holds a central and profound significance. Often described as the life force that animates all living beings and permeates the universe, energy is the fundamental building block of magical workings, rituals, and spells. Understanding how to access and channel this hidden power is essential for practitioners seeking to harness its transformative potential and manifest their intentions into reality. Through various techniques and practices, practitioners can tap into the vast reservoirs of energy surrounding them, harnessing its power to establish positive change in their lives and the world around them.

One of the key principles underlying the practice of accessing and channeling energy is the recognition that energy is omnipresent and abundant in the universe. From the subtle vibrations of the air to the magnetic fields of the earth, energy constantly flows and circulates throughout the cosmos, animating all forms of life and matter. By attuning themselves to the rhythms and vibrations of the universe, practitioners can tap into this vast reservoir of energy, harnessing its power to fuel their magical workings and manifest their intentions with greater clarity and effectiveness.

Furthermore, practitioners must develop a strong sense of awareness and presence in the present moment in order to access and channel energy. Energy follows attention, therefore practitioners can channel the flow of energy in the direction of their ambitions by concentrating their awareness and purpose on the intended result of their magical operations. Through practices such as meditation, visualization, and mindfulness, practitioners can quiet the mind's chatter, center themselves in the present moment, and attune themselves to the subtle energies surrounding them, allowing them to access and channel energy with greater ease and precision.

Furthermore, accessing and channeling energy involves cultivating sensitivity and receptivity to the subtle nuances of energetic vibrations. Energy manifests in various forms and frequencies, ranging from the gentle hum of the earth to the intense heat of fire, and practitioners must learn to discern and work with these energies in their magical practice. By honing their intuitive abilities and deepening their connection to the natural world, practitioners can attune themselves to the subtle vibrations of energy, allowing them to sense its presence, flow, and quality with greater clarity and accuracy.

In addition, accessing and channeling energy requires practitioners to cultivate a sense of balance and harmony within themselves and with the energies they seek to work with. Energy is neither inherently good nor bad—it is neutral and can be influenced by the intentions and actions of individuals. By cultivating virtues such as integrity, compassion, and respect in their magical practice, practitioners can ensure that they work with energy responsibly and ethically, aligning their intentions with higher principles and values. Through practices such as grounding, centering, and shielding, practitioners can create a protective barrier around themselves, shielding them from negative energies and ensuring they work with energy in a safe and supportive environment.

Moreover, accessing and channeling energy involves cultivating skill and mastery over various techniques and practices. From manipulating energy through visualization and intention to using tools such as wands, crystals, and incense, practitioners employ an array of techniques to access and channel energy in their magical workings. Through study, practice, and experimentation, practitioners can refine their skills and deepen their understanding of how to work with energy, allowing them to manifest their intentions with greater precision and effectiveness.

In conclusion, accessing and channeling energy is a foundational aspect of magical practice, allowing practitioners to tap into the vast energy reservoirs surrounding them and manifest their intentions into reality. By cultivating awareness, sensitivity, and receptivity to the subtle vibrations of energy, practitioners can attune themselves to its flow and quality, harnessing its power to create positive change in their lives and in the world around them. Through practices such as meditation, visualization, and mindfulness, practitioners can access and channel energy with greater ease and precision, leading to profound shifts in consciousness and manifestation. Thus, by unveiling the hidden power of energy, practitioners can unlock their fullest potential as magicians and co-creators of their own destiny.

Cultivating Personal Power through Magical Practice

Magical practice offers individuals a unique and potent pathway to cultivate personal power—a sense of inner strength, sovereignty, and agency that empowers them to manifest their intentions and shape their reality according to their desires. Unlike traditional forms of power that may be based on external factors including wealth, status, or authority, personal power in the context of magical practice is rooted in one's connection to the divine, the natural world, and the depths of their own being. By harnessing the energies of the universe and tapping into the depths of their own consciousness, practitioners can cultivate personal power in an authentic, empowering way, and aligned with their highest values and aspirations.

One of the primary ways in which magical practice cultivates personal power is by facilitating a deep and intimate connection to the divine forces of the universe. Whether one conceptualizes the divine as God, Goddess, spirit, or universal consciousness, magical practice offers individuals a direct and experiential connection to the divine that transcends traditional religious frameworks and dogmas. Through practices such as ritual, prayer, meditation, and communion with nature, practitioners can tap into the divine energies that flow through all of creation, aligning themselves with the higher wisdom and guidance of the universe. By forging a personal relationship with the divine, practitioners can draw upon its infinite power and wisdom to support and empower them on their spiritual journey, leading to a profound sense of personal power and sovereignty.

Moreover, magical practice cultivates personal power by fostering a deep as well as intimate connection to the natural world. Nature is a potent source of energy, wisdom, and healing, and by attuning themselves to its rhythms and cycles, practitioners can tap into its regenerative power and vitality. Whether through practices such as grounding, communing with plants and animals, or working with the elements, practitioners can deepen their connection to the natural world and draw upon its energies to support and empower them on their spiritual journey. By aligning themselves with the natural rhythms and cycles of the earth, practitioners can harness its transformative power to manifest their intentions with greater ease and effectiveness, leading to a profound sense of personal power and connection to the web of life.

Furthermore, magical practice cultivates personal power by empowering individuals to tap into the depths of their own consciousness and unlock their hidden potentials. The human mind is a vast and mysterious landscape, filled with untapped reservoirs of creativity, intuition, and insight. Through practices such as meditation, visualization, and inner journeying, practitioners can explore the depths of their own consciousness, uncovering the hidden truths and potentials that lie within. By delving into the depths of their own psyche, practitioners can overcome limiting beliefs, fears, and self-doubt, unlocking their fullest potential and harnessing their personal power to create positive change in their lives and in the world around them.

In addition, magical practice cultivates personal power by providing individuals with a framework for self-discovery, growth, and transformation. Through practices such as ritual, spellcraft, and energy work, practitioners can engage in a process of inner alchemy, transmuting their fears, doubts, and limitations into sources of strength, resilience, and empowerment. By confronting their shadows and embracing their light, practitioners can integrate all aspects of themselves into a coherent and harmonious whole, leading to a profound sense of personal power and authenticity. Through the process of self-discovery and growth, practitioners can develop a deep sense of self-awareness and self-acceptance, empowering them to live authentically and manifest their true desires with confidence and clarity.

Moreover, magical practice cultivates personal power by fostering a sense of community and belonging among practitioners. Magic is a profoundly communal and collaborative endeavor, and by working together with like-minded individuals, practitioners can amplify their intentions and manifest their desires with greater ease and effectiveness. Whether through group rituals, coven work, or online communities, practitioners can connect with others who share their values and aspirations, drawing upon their collective energy and wisdom to support and empower each other on their spiritual journey. By cultivating a sense of community and belonging, practitioners can tap into the group's collective power, leading to a profound sense of personal power and connection to something greater than themselves.

In conclusion, magical practice offers individuals a powerful pathway to cultivate personal power—a sense of inner strength, sovereignty, and agency that empowers them to manifest their intentions and shape their reality according to their desires. By forging a deep and intimate connection to the divine, the natural world, and the depths of their own being, practitioners can tap into vast reservoirs of energy, wisdom, and creativity that lie within and around them. Through practices such as ritual, meditation, and inner journeying, practitioners can unlock their hidden potentials, transcend their limitations, and harness their personal power to create positive change in their lives and in the world around them. Thus, by cultivating personal power through magical practice, individuals can awaken to their true potential and live authentically as empowered co-creators of their own destiny.

CHAPTER IV

The Alchemical Process

Philosophical Foundations of Alchemy

Alchemy, the ancient art and science of transmutation, has deep philosophical roots that trace back to antiquity and span across diverse cultural and spiritual traditions. At its core, alchemy is not merely concerned with the physical transformation of base metals into gold, but with the metaphorical journey of inner transformation and spiritual enlightenment. The philosophical foundations of alchemy are multifaceted, drawing inspiration from Greek, Egyptian, Hermetic, and Gnostic philosophies, among others, to create a rich tapestry of mystical wisdom that continues to fascinate and inspire seekers of truth and wisdom.

One of the central philosophical principles of alchemy is the concept of "As above, so below; as within, so without." This principle, often attributed to Hermes Trismegistus, the legendary founder of Hermeticism, reflects the belief that the microcosm of the individual reflects the macrocosm of the universe, and vice versa. In other words, the processes of transformation and evolution that occur within the human psyche are mirrored in the natural world and the cosmos at large. By understanding and working with these correspondences, alchemists seek to unlock the universe's secrets and harness its transformative energies for personal and spiritual growth.

Another foundational principle of alchemy is the idea of the prima materia, or the "first matter," from which all things are believed to arise. In alchemical symbolism, the prima materia is often depicted as a chaotic and formless substance that contains the seeds of potentiality and transformation. Through the process of alchemical work, the prima materia is subjected to various operations and transformations, ultimately leading to the emergence of the philosopher's stone—the symbol of spiritual enlightenment and immortality. The quest for the philosopher's stone represents the alchemist's journey of self-discovery and inner transformation, as they seek to transmute the base elements of their psyche into gold.

The notion of the alchemical wedding is central to the philosophical foundations of alchemy—the union of opposites and the integration of polarities within the psyche. Drawing on the ancient Greek concept of the coincidentia oppositorum, or the unity of opposites, alchemy seeks to reconcile the dualities of light and darkness, masculine and feminine, conscious and unconscious, within the individual. Through the process of inner alchemy, the alchemist seeks to harmonize these opposing forces, transcending the limitations of the ego and attaining union with the divine. This process of integration is symbolized by the alchemical wedding, where the alchemist becomes a vessel for the divine union of spirit and matter, heaven and earth.

Furthermore, alchemy is deeply influenced by Neoplatonic philosophy, which posits the existence of a transcendent realm of pure forms or archetypes that underlie physical reality. According to Neoplatonism, the material world is but a reflection or shadow of these higher realities, and the goal of spiritual practice is to ascend through the levels of being to reunite with the divine source. Alchemy, emphasizing the transmutation of matter and spirit, echoes the Neoplatonic vision of spiritual ascent, as the alchemist seeks to purify and refine the material world to reveal its underlying spiritual essence.

In addition to these philosophical influences, alchemy is also shaped by the mystical traditions of Kabbalah, Gnosticism, and Eastern spirituality, which provide further insights into the nature of reality and the human soul. Kabbalistic teachings on the Tree of Life, for example, offer a symbolic framework for understanding the process of spiritual evolution and the dynamics of the psyche. Gnostic myths and symbols, such as the ouroboros (the serpent eating its own tail) and the phoenix (the bird of resurrection), provide powerful metaphors for the cyclical nature of existence and the possibility of spiritual rebirth and regeneration.

In conclusion, the philosophical foundations of alchemy are vast and diverse, drawing on a rich tapestry of wisdom from ancient and esoteric traditions. From the Hermetic principle of correspondence to the Neoplatonic vision of spiritual ascent, from the alchemical wedding of opposites to the mystical insights of Kabbalah and Gnosticism, alchemy offers a profound synthesis of philosophical, spiritual, and metaphysical teachings that continue to motivate seekers of truth and wisdom to this day.
Through the practice of alchemy, individuals embark on a journey of self-discovery and inner transformation, seeking to unlock the secrets of the universe and awaken to their true potential as divine beings.

Transmutation: Turning Base Desires into Noble Goals

Transmutation, the alchemical process of transforming base metals into gold, is a powerful metaphor for the spiritual journey of turning base desires into noble goals. In the mystical tradition of alchemy, gold symbolizes material wealth, spiritual enlightenment, and inner wisdom. Likewise, base desires represent the lower, instinctual urges of the ego, while noble goals embody the higher aspirations of the soul. The alchemical journey of transmutation involves purifying and refining the raw materials of the psyche, harnessing the transformative power of desire to propel oneself towards higher states of consciousness and self-realization.

At the heart of transmutation lies the recognition that all desires, whether base or noble, originate from the same source—the human heart. Desire, with its primal energy and creative force, is neither inherently good nor bad but it can be directed towards constructive or destructive ends depending on how it is cultivated and channeled. The alchemist seeks to harness the energies of desire, purifying them of impurities and aligning them with the higher principles of truth, beauty, and virtue. This process of transmutation requires self-awareness, discipline, and a willingness to confront and transform the shadow aspects of the psyche.

One of the critical principles of transmutation is the alchemical wedding—the union of opposites within the individual. This union integrates the polarities of light and darkness, masculine and feminine, conscious and unconscious, into a harmonious whole. By reconciling these dualities within the psyche, the alchemist transcends the limitations of the ego and attains a state of inner balance and wholeness. This integration process is essential for transmuting base desires into noble goals, as it enables the individual to align their intentions and actions with their highest ideals and values.

Furthermore, transmutation involves the cultivation of virtues such as patience, perseverance, and compassion. The alchemical process is often fraught with challenges and setbacks, requiring the alchemist to navigate the depths of their own psyche and confront the obstacles that stand in the way of their spiritual growth. By cultivating virtues such as patience, the alchemist learns to endure the trials and tribulations of the journey with grace and resilience. By cultivating virtues such as perseverance, the alchemist learns to persist in their quest for self-transformation despite setbacks and obstacles. And by cultivating virtues such as compassion, the alchemist learns to approach themselves and others with kindness and understanding, recognizing all beings' inherent dignity and worth.

Moreover, transmutation involves the cultivation of mindfulness and presence in the present moment. The alchemist learns to observe their thoughts, feelings, and sensations with detached awareness, recognizing that their desires or identities do not define them. By cultivating mindfulness, the alchemist learns to break free from the grasp of unconscious patterns and conditioning, allowing them to respond to life's challenges with clarity and wisdom. By cultivating presence, the alchemist learns to fully inhabit the present moment, recognizing that true fulfillment and meaning are found not in pursuing external goals but in the experience of the here and now.

In conclusion, transmutation is a profound journey of self-discovery and self-realization, in which base desires are transformed into noble goals through the alchemical process of purification and refinement. The alchemist embarks on a transformative journey towards higher states of consciousness and spiritual enlightenment by harnessing the energies of desire, integrating the polarities of the psyche, cultivating virtues such as patience and compassion, and practicing mindfulness and presence. In the end, the true gold of the alchemical journey is not found in material wealth or external success, but in the realization of one's true nature as a divine being and the embodiment of love, wisdom, and compassion.

Balancing Desire and Power: The Middle Path of Alchemy

In the mystical tradition of alchemy, the quest for spiritual enlightenment and transformation is often described as a journey of balancing desire and power—the twin forces that drive human behavior and shape the course of our lives. At its core, alchemy teaches that desire, with its inherent energy and creative force, is the driving force behind our progress on the path to self-realization and self-discovery. Yet, unchecked desire can lead to imbalance and suffering, as we become consumed by the relentless pursuit of external gratification and lose sight of our deeper purpose and meaning in life. Likewise, power, with its capacity to influence, control, and shape the world around us, is a potent tool for manifesting our intentions and achieving our goals. However, power wielded without wisdom and integrity can lead to corruption and abuse, as we become intoxicated by our own sense of importance and lose touch with our ethical and moral compass.

The alchemical tradition offers a path of balance and harmony—a middle way that integrates the energies of desire and power in service of higher ideals and spiritual growth. This middle path is rooted in the principle of moderation—the recognition that neither excessive indulgence nor complete renunciation of desire and power leads to lasting fulfillment and happiness. Instead, the alchemist seeks to cultivate a balanced relationship with desire and power, harnessing their energies with wisdom, discernment, and ethical integrity. This involves cultivating self-awareness and self-mastery, learning to recognize and regulate the impulses of the ego, and aligning one's actions with the principles of truth, beauty, and virtue.

One of the key teachings of the middle path of alchemy is the principle of detachment—the ability to cultivate desire without being consumed by it. Detachment does not mean suppressing or denying our desires, but rather observing them with mindful awareness and discerning which desires are conducive to our spiritual growth and well-being. By cultivating detachment, the alchemist learns to free themselves from the grip of craving and attachment, allowing them to pursue their goals with clarity and purpose, without being driven by the ego's dictates. This enables the alchemist to cultivate a more profound sense of inner freedom and autonomy, as they become less reliant on external circumstances and conditions for their happiness and fulfillment.

Furthermore, the middle path of alchemy involves cultivating humility and humility, recognizing that true power arises not from the domination of others but from the alignment of one's will with the divine will. Humility involves acknowledging our limitations and imperfections, and recognizing that we are but humble servants of a greater cosmic order. By cultivating humility, the alchemist learns to approach power with reverence and respect, recognizing its sacred nature and using it to serve the highest good. Similarly, humility involves acknowledging the contributions and perspectives of others and recognizing that true wisdom arises from a diversity of voices and experiences. By cultivating humility, the alchemist learns to listen deeply to the wisdom of others and to collaborate with them in pursuing shared goals and aspirations.

Moreover, the middle path of alchemy involves cultivating compassion and empathy towards oneself and others. Compassion involves recognizing all beings' inherent dignity and worth and responding to their suffering with kindness and understanding. By cultivating compassion, the alchemist learns to approach themselves and others with gentleness and compassion, recognizing that we are all fellow travelers on life's journey, seeking happiness and fulfillment in our own unique ways. Similarly, empathy involves stepping into the shoes of others and seeing the world from their perspective, recognizing that we are all interconnected and interdependent. By cultivating empathy, the alchemist learns to bridge the divides that separate us and to build bridges of understanding and solidarity with others.

In conclusion, the middle path of alchemy offers a profound path of balance and harmony, in which desire and power are harnessed with wisdom, discernment, and ethical integrity. By cultivating detachment, humility, compassion, and empathy, the alchemist learns to navigate the complexities of desire and power with grace and dignity, aligning their actions with the highest ideals of truth, beauty, and virtue. In embracing the middle path of alchemy, we awaken to our true nature as divine beings, capable of harnessing the energies of desire and power in service of the greater good and the highest good of all beings.

Harnessing Desire as a Catalyst for Magical Change

Desire, with its fiery and relentless nature, has long been recognized as a powerful catalyst for change in the realm of magic. It drives intentions, rituals, and spells, fueling the practitioner's will and propelling their magical workings toward manifestation. When harnessed effectively, desire becomes a potent tool for transformation, allowing practitioners to tap into their deepest longings and manifest their intentions with clarity and purpose.

At its core, desire is the fuel that ignites the flame of intention in magical practice. Intentions are the conscious thoughts and wishes that practitioners seek to manifest through their magical workings, and desire is the driving force that propels these intentions into reality. The intensity and clarity of one's desire directly influence the energy and momentum behind their intentions, making it crucial for practitioners to cultivate a deep and focused desire for their desired outcomes. By aligning their desires with their intentions and infusing them with passion and conviction, practitioners can amplify the energy behind their magical workings, increasing their likelihood of success and manifestation.

Moreover, desire is a powerful catalyst for magical change by providing practitioners with a clear and compelling vision of the future they wish to create. When individuals strongly desire something—a goal, aspiration, or dream—they are often motivated to take action and make changes in their lives to bring it to fruition. In magical practice, desire is a beacon of light that guides practitioners toward their desired outcomes, inspiring them to take the necessary steps and make the required sacrifices to manifest their intentions. By harnessing the power of desire to create a clear and compelling vision of their goals, practitioners can align their thoughts, emotions, and actions with their intentions, increasing their chances of success and manifestation.

Furthermore, desire catalyzes magical change by tapping into the subconscious mind and uncovering hidden truths and potentials within. The subconscious mind is the repository of our deepest desires, fears, and beliefs, influencing our thoughts, emotions, and behaviors in subtle and often unseen ways. By tapping into the power of desire, practitioners can access the wisdom as well as guidance of the subconscious mind, gaining insights into the underlying motivations and needs driving their magical workings. Through practices such as visualization, meditation, and dreamwork, practitioners can explore the depths of their subconscious mind, uncovering hidden truths and unlocking the secrets of their innermost selves. By harnessing the power of desire to connect with the subconscious mind, practitioners can deepen their understanding of themselves and their magical practice, leading to profound shifts in consciousness and self-awareness.

In addition, desire catalyzes magical change by facilitating the process of manifestation and transformation. Manifestation is the process of bringing one's desires and intentions into physical form, turning abstract thoughts and ideas into tangible reality. By harnessing the power of desire, practitioners can align their thoughts, emotions, and actions with their intentions, increasing the energy and momentum behind their magical workings and accelerating the manifestation process. Whether through rituals, spells, or affirmations, practitioners can use desire as a catalyst to channel their intentions into the universe, allowing them to manifest their desires with greater speed and effectiveness.

Moreover, desire catalyzes magical change by empowering practitioners to overcome obstacles and challenges on their spiritual journey. The path of magic is not always easy, and practitioners may encounter numerous obstacles and setbacks along the way. However, when fueled by a deep and unwavering desire for their goals, practitioners can overcome even the most formidable challenges, tapping into their inner strength as well as resilience to persevere in the face of adversity. By harnessing the power of desire to fuel their determination and commitment, practitioners can navigate the ups and downs of their spiritual journey with grace and fortitude, leading to profound growth and transformation.

In conclusion, desire is a powerful catalyst for magical change, fueling the practitioner's will and propelling their intentions toward manifestation. When harnessed effectively, desire becomes a potent tool for transformation, allowing practitioners to tap into their deepest longings and manifest their intentions with clarity and purpose. By aligning their desires with their intentions, practitioners can amplify the energy behind their magical workings, increase their chances of success and manifestation, and navigate the challenges of their spiritual journey with grace and fortitude. Thus, by harnessing desire as a catalyst for magical change, practitioners can unlock their fullest potential and establish positive change in their lives and in the world around them.

Case Studies: Examples of Desire-Alchemy in Magical Traditions

Throughout history, magical traditions worldwide have incorporated the concept of desire-alchemy—the transformation of desires into tangible reality—into their practices. These traditions recognize the potent power of desire as a catalyst for change and have developed various techniques and rituals to harness this power and manifest intentions with precision and effectiveness. By examining case studies from different magical traditions, we can gain insights into how practitioners have utilized desire-alchemy to create positive change in their lives and in the world around them.

One prominent example of desire-alchemy in magical traditions is found in the practice of ceremonial magic, particularly within the Western occult tradition. Ceremonial magicians often work with elaborate rituals, symbols, and invocations to invoke and channel divine energies for specific purposes. In these rituals, practitioners cultivate a deep and focused desire for their desired outcomes, aligning their intentions with the energies of the cosmos and directing them toward manifestation. Through practices such as sigil magic, evocation, and astral projection, practitioners can tap into the vast reservoirs of energy surrounding them, harnessing its power to manifest their intentions with precision and effectiveness.

Another example of desire-alchemy can be found in the practice of chaos magic, a modern magical tradition that emphasizes experimentation, flexibility, and personalization. Chaos magicians employ various techniques and practices drawn from various magical traditions, adapting them to suit their individual needs and preferences. In chaos magic, practitioners often work with sigils—personalized symbols that represent their desires—and employ techniques such as gnosis and trance induction to imbue them with energy and intent. By focusing their desire on the sigil and charging it with energy, practitioners can send their intentions out into the universe, allowing them to manifest in unexpected and miraculous ways.

Furthermore, desire-alchemy is central to the practice of sympathetic magic, a magical tradition that operates on the principle of "like attracts like." Sympathetic magicians believe that by creating symbolic representations of their desires and manipulating them in ritualistic ways, they can influence the corresponding aspects of reality. For example, practitioners may create effigies, talismans, or potions to represent their desires and perform rituals to activate them. By imbuing these symbolic representations with their focused desire and intention, practitioners can harness the power of sympathetic magic to manifest their intentions with precision and effectiveness.

Additionally, desire-alchemy is integral to the practice of tantra, an esoteric tradition that seeks to harness the power of desire and sexual energy for spiritual transformation. Tantric practitioners believe that when directed with intention and awareness, desire can be a potent force for awakening consciousness and achieving enlightenment. Through practices such as mantra, visualization, and ritualized sex, practitioners can harness the energy of desire to awaken the dormant potentials within themselves, leading to profound spiritual awakening and transformation.

In conclusion, desire-alchemy is a central and universal concept in magical traditions, representing the transformation of desires into tangible reality through focused intention and ritualistic practice. By examining case studies from different magical traditions, we can see how practitioners have utilized desire-alchemy to create positive change in their lives and in the world around them. Whether through ceremonial magic, chaos magic, sympathetic magic, or tantra, practitioners have developed various techniques and practices to harness the power of desire and manifest their intentions with precision and effectiveness. Thus, desire-alchemy remains a potent and indispensable tool for practitioners seeking to create positive change in their lives and unlock their fullest potential through magic.

CHAPTER V

Techniques of Transformation

Rituals for Awakening Desire

Desire, with its primal energy and creative force, lies at the heart of the human experience, driving us to pursue our dreams, fulfill our aspirations, and seek fulfillment in life. Yet, desire is a multifaceted phenomenon that can be both a source of inspiration and a source of suffering, depending on how it is cultivated and expressed. Rituals for awakening desire offer a sacred and intentional approach to harnessing the power of desire, allowing us to connect with our deepest longings and aspirations and channel them towards meaningful and transformative ends. These rituals draw upon ancient wisdom traditions, mystical practices, and psychological insights to create a sacred container for exploring and cultivating desire, guiding us on a journey of self-discovery, empowerment, as well as spiritual growth.

One of the key elements of rituals for awakening desire is intention setting—the conscious and deliberate articulation of our desires and intentions. Intention setting involves clarifying what we truly desire and why it is important to us, as well as visualizing and affirming our intentions with conviction and faith. This process of intention setting helps to focus our energy as well as attention on what truly matters to us, aligning our thoughts, feelings, and actions with our deepest aspirations and values. Rituals for awakening desire often incorporate various symbolic elements, such as candles, incense, sacred objects, and imagery, to create a sacred space and evoke a sense of reverence and awe.

Another essential element of rituals for awakening desire is embodiment—the process of connecting with our desires on a physical, emotional, and energetic level. Embodiment practices such as movement, breathwork, and somatic awareness help to ground our desires in the present moment and anchor them in our bodies. By tuning into the sensations and feelings that arise within us, we can deepen our connection to our desires and access the wisdom of our bodies as a source of guidance and insight. Embodiment practices also help to release any blocks or resistance that may hinder the free flow of desire, allowing us to experience greater vitality, aliveness, and empowerment.

Moreover, rituals for awakening desire often incorporate elements of ceremony and symbolism to evoke a sense of sacredness and reverence for the mystery and wonder of life. Ceremonial rituals such as lighting candles, offering prayers, chanting mantras, and invoking divine guidance help to create a sacred container for the exploration and expression of desire, inviting the participation of higher forces and spiritual allies in our journey of awakening. Symbolic rituals such as creating altars, crafting talismans, and performing symbolic gestures help to externalize and concretize our desires, making them tangible and real in the physical world. Through these rituals, we honor the sacredness of desire and affirm our commitment to its cultivation and expression.

Additionally, rituals for awakening desire often incorporate storytelling and mythic imagery elements to tap into the collective unconscious and access the archetypal dimensions of desire. Mythic narratives such as the hero's journey, the quest for the Holy Grail, and the alchemical wedding are potent symbols of the human journey of awakening desire, inspiring us to embark on our own quest for self-discovery and transformation. By immersing ourselves in these stories and symbols, we can access deeper layers of meaning and insight into the nature of desire and its role in our lives. Rituals for awakening desire also provide opportunities for creative expression and exploration, allowing us to tap into our innate creativity and imagination as a source of inspiration and empowerment.

In conclusion, rituals for awakening desire offer a sacred and intentional approach to harnessing the power of desire for personal and spiritual growth. By setting clear intentions, embodying our desires, engaging in ceremonial practices, and tapping into the wisdom of mythic narratives, we can cultivate a deeper connection to our desires and channel their transformative energy towards meaningful and fulfilling ends. These rituals provide a sacred space for exploring and expressing desire, inviting us to embrace the fullness of our humanity and awaken to the infinite possibilities that lie within us.

Spells and Charms for Channeling Power

In the mystical realm of magic and witchcraft, spells and charms are potent tools for channeling and harnessing power to manifest intentions, protect against harm, and invoke blessings. Rooted in ancient wisdom traditions and passed down through generations, spells and charms draw upon the natural energies of the universe to make change and influence the course of events. These magical practices are grounded in the belief that everything in the cosmos is interconnected and imbued with divine energy, and that by tapping into this energy, practitioners can manipulate reality to achieve their desires.

Spells are rituals performed with specific intentions, often involving spoken or written incantations, symbolic gestures, and ritual tools such as candles, herbs, crystals, and sigils. Each element of a spell is carefully chosen and imbued with meaning, focusing and amplifying the practitioner's intentions and energy. Spells can be used for different purposes, including attracting love and prosperity, banishing negativity and obstacles, healing physical and emotional ailments, and enhancing psychic abilities and intuition. The effectiveness of a spell often depends on factors such as the practitioner's skill and concentration, the alignment of planetary energies, and the potency of the materials used.

Charms, on the other hand, are objects imbued with magical properties that are carried or worn as talismans for protection, luck, and empowerment. Charms can take many forms, including amulets, pendants, rings, and sachets, and are often crafted from materials such as metals, stones, herbs, and animal parts. Each charm is believed to possess its own unique vibration and energy signature, which resonates with specific intentions and qualities. For example, a silver pentacle pendant may be worn for protection against negative energies, while a green aventurine stone may be carried for attracting wealth and abundance. Charms are often consecrated and charged with magical energy through rituals and prayers, infusing them with the power to manifest desired outcomes.

The process of casting spells and crafting charms involves tapping into the elemental energies of earth, air, fire, and water and the subtle energies of spirit and ether. Practitioners may call upon the elemental forces to lend their strength and support to the spell or charm, invoking the qualities of each element to enhance its effectiveness. For example, earth energy may be invoked for grounding and stability, air energy for communication and clarity, fire energy for passion and transformation, and water energy for emotional healing and intuition. By working in harmony with the elements, practitioners can amplify the power of their spells and charms and align them with the natural rhythms of the universe.

In addition to elemental energies, spells and charms often incorporate correspondences from astrology, numerology, and other esoteric systems to enhance their potency and efficacy. For example, practitioners may time their spells and rituals to coincide with specific planetary alignments or lunar phases, harnessing the energies of the cosmos to support their intentions. Similarly, practitioners may use numerological correspondences to determine the most auspicious times for casting spells and crafting charms, based on the vibrational qualities of different numbers. By aligning their magical practices with these cosmic influences, practitioners can amplify the power of their spells and charms and increase the likelihood of success.

Furthermore, spells and charms are often imbued with symbolic meanings and associations drawn from mythology, folklore, and cultural traditions. These symbols are potent archetypes that resonate with the collective unconscious, evoking deep-seated emotions and desires within the practitioner's psyche. For example, a spell invoking the image of the moon may tap into the archetypal energies of intuition, mystery, and transformation, while a charm depicting a serpent may symbolize rebirth, healing, and wisdom. By working with these symbolic images and associations, practitioners can access the deeper layers of their unconscious mind and harness the power of the collective imagination to manifest their intentions.

In conclusion, spells and charms are potent tools for channeling and harnessing magical power to create change and influence the course of events. Rooted in ancient wisdom traditions and passed down through generations, spells and charms draw upon the natural energies of the universe and the elemental forces of earth, air, fire, and water to manifest intentions and achieve desired outcomes. By working with symbolic imagery, elemental energies, and correspondences from astrology, numerology, and mythology, practitioners can amplify the potency of their spells and charms and align them with the natural rhythms of the cosmos. Through the practice of casting spells and crafting charms, practitioners tap into the deep well of magical energy that lies within them, empowering themselves to manifest their desires as well as shape their reality according to their will.

Meditation and Visualization Exercises for Alchemical Integration

Meditation and visualization exercises are powerful tools for achieving inner transformation and spiritual integration in the alchemical tradition. Rooted in ancient wisdom traditions and esoteric practices, these techniques are designed to awaken dormant potentials within the psyche, cultivate self-awareness, and facilitate the alchemical process of transmutation—the transformation of the leaden aspects of the self into the golden qualities of enlightenment and spiritual awakening. Through regular practice, practitioners can tap into the deep well of inner wisdom and intuitive knowing that lies within them, unlocking the secrets of the soul and accessing higher states of consciousness.

Meditation is a foundational practice in the alchemical tradition, offering a direct path to inner stillness, clarity, and insight. By quieting the mind and also turning inward, practitioners can observe the movements of their thoughts, emotions, and sensations with detached awareness, cultivating a deep sense of presence and inner peace. Meditation techniques such as mindfulness meditation, concentration meditation, and loving-kindness meditation help to cultivate different aspects of awareness and attention, enabling practitioners to develop greater clarity, focus, and stability in their lives. Through regular meditation practice, practitioners can cultivate the inner spaciousness and stillness necessary for deep self-reflection and inner transformation.

Visualization exercises are another essential aspect of alchemical practice, allowing practitioners to harness the power of imagination and creative visualization to evoke inner states of consciousness and effect positive change in their lives. Visualization techniques such as guided imagery, symbolic visualization, and journeying help to activate the subconscious mind and access deeper layers of the psyche, where unconscious patterns and conditioning reside. By visualizing specific images, symbols, or scenes, practitioners can evoke feelings of empowerment, healing, and spiritual awakening, catalyzing the process of inner transformation and integration. Visualization exercises are often combined with meditation practices to enhance the experience's effectiveness.

One of the key principles of alchemical integration is the alchemical wedding—the union of opposites within the psyche. Visualization exercises can help practitioners to explore and integrate the polarities of light and darkness, masculine and feminine, conscious and unconscious, within themselves. By visualizing symbolic images or scenes that represent these polarities, practitioners can cultivate a sense of inner balance and harmony, transcending the limitations of the ego and attaining a state of wholeness and integration. For example, practitioners may visualize themselves standing at the crossroads of light and darkness, embodying both qualities within themselves and experiencing the transformative power of their union.

Furthermore, visualization exercises can help practitioners to work with archetypal symbols and mythic imagery from the alchemical tradition, tapping into the collective unconscious and accessing deeper layers of meaning and insight. By visualizing images such as the alchemical symbols of the sun and moon, the philosopher's stone, or the ouroboros (the serpent eating its own tail), practitioners can evoke the archetypal energies of transformation, rebirth, and spiritual awakening. These symbols serve as potent gateways to the deeper mysteries of the soul, guiding practitioners on their journey of self-discovery and inner transformation.

In addition to visualization exercises, practitioners may also engage in guided meditations and journeys led by experienced facilitators or teachers. These guided experiences provide a structured framework for exploring the inner realms of consciousness and accessing higher states of awareness. Guided meditations may involve visualization exercises, breathwork, and body awareness techniques, as well as storytelling, music, and ritual elements to enhance the experience. By surrendering to the guidance of a professional facilitator, practitioners can deepen their meditation practice and access more profound levels of insight and wisdom.

In conclusion, meditation and visualization exercises are powerful tools for alchemical integration, offering a direct path to inner transformation and spiritual awakening. By cultivating inner stillness, clarity, and presence through meditation, practitioners can create the conditions necessary for deep self-reflection and inner healing. Through visualization exercises, practitioners can tap into the power of imagination and creative visualization to evoke inner states of consciousness and effect positive change in their lives. By working with archetypal symbols, mythic imagery, and guided experiences, practitioners can access deeper layers of meaning and insight, guiding them on their journey of self-discovery and inner transformation. Through regular practice and dedication, practitioners can unlock the secrets of the soul and awaken to their true potential as divine beings.

Creating Personalized Rituals for Alchemical Transformation

Rituals are the cornerstone of magical practice, serving as powerful tools for harnessing the universe's energies and manifesting intentions into reality. In the context of alchemical transformation, rituals play a crucial role in facilitating inner change, growth, and evolution on both a personal and spiritual level. By creating personalized rituals tailored to their unique needs, desires, and aspirations, practitioners can tap into the transformative power of magic to catalyze profound shifts in consciousness and manifest their true potential.

One of the vital principles underlying the creation of personalized rituals for alchemical transformation is the recognition that each individual's journey is unique and sacred. No two practitioners are alike, and what may work for one person may not resonate with another. Therefore, practitioners need to take the time to reflect on their own desires, intentions, and goals before crafting a ritual that is tailored to their specific needs and aspirations. By aligning their rituals with their deepest longings and intentions, practitioners can create a sacred space for transformation to unfold, allowing them to tap into the limitless potential of their own being.

Moreover, personalized rituals for alchemical transformation often involve a combination of elements drawn from various magical traditions, practices, and modalities. Practitioners may incorporate elements such as meditation, visualization, energy work, and ceremonial magic into their rituals, adapting them to suit their individual preferences and needs. By drawing upon diverse techniques and practices, practitioners can create a holistic and multidimensional ritual experience that addresses all aspects of their being—physical, emotional, mental, and spiritual. This integrated approach allows practitioners to work with the universe's energies on multiple levels, facilitating more profound transformation.

Furthermore, personalized rituals for alchemical transformation are often imbued with symbolism and meaning that is personally significant to the practitioner. Symbols can evoke deep emotions, memories, and insights, serving as potent catalysts for inner change and growth. By incorporating symbols that resonate with their intentions and aspirations into their rituals, practitioners can tap into the collective unconscious and access the wisdom and guidance of their higher selves. Whether through the use of sacred objects, imagery, or words of power, practitioners can infuse their rituals with symbolism and meaning that speaks directly to their soul, deepening their connection to the transformative energies at work.

In addition, personalized rituals for alchemical transformation often involve the creation of sacred space—a consecrated space where practitioners can connect with the energies of the divine and the natural world. Creating sacred space involves purifying and consecrating the physical environment, as well as invoking divine energies and guardians to protect and guide the ritual. By creating a sacred space for their rituals, practitioners can amplify the energy and intention behind their workings, creating a powerful container for transformation to unfold. This sacred space serves as a gateway between the mundane and the divine, allowing practitioners to commune with the forces of the universe and manifest their intentions with clarity and purpose.

Moreover, personalized rituals for alchemical transformation often incorporate elements of self-care and self-love into their practice. Transformation is a process that requires patience, compassion, and gentleness with oneself, and practitioners must take the time to nurture and nourish themselves on all levels—

physically, emotionally, mentally, and spiritually. By incorporating elements such as aromatherapy, massage, journaling, and affirmations into their rituals, practitioners can create a supportive and nurturing environment for transformation to unfold, allowing them to release old patterns and embrace new possibilities with grace and ease.

In conclusion, personalized rituals for alchemical transformation are powerful tools for harnessing the universe's energies and manifesting intentions into reality. By crafting rituals that are tailored to their unique needs, desires, and aspirations, practitioners can tap into the transformative power of magic to catalyze profound shifts in consciousness and manifest their true potential. Whether through meditation, visualization, energy work, or ceremonial magic, personalized rituals offer practitioners a sacred space for transformation to unfold, allowing them to connect with the deepest longing of their soul and create positive change in their lives and the world around them. Thus, by embracing the power of personalized rituals for alchemical transformation, practitioners can unlock their fullest potential and awaken to the limitless possibilities of their own being.

CHAPTER VI

Exploring the Elemental Forces

Earth: Grounding Desire in Reality

In the alchemical tradition, the element of Earth is the foundation upon which all transformation occurs. Earth is associated with stability, grounding, and material manifestation, serving as the physical container through which the energies of desire are channeled and expressed. Grounding desire in reality requires cultivating a deep connection to the element of Earth, anchoring our aspirations and intentions in the tangible realm of the physical world. This grounding process involves attuning ourselves to the rhythms of nature, honoring the cycles of growth and decay, and aligning our desires with the natural order of the universe.

At its essence, grounding desire in reality is about bringing our dreams and aspirations down to earth, making them tangible and achievable within the constraints of our physical existence. This requires clarity of vision, practicality, and willingness to roll up our sleeves and do the necessary work to manifest our desires. Grounding desire in reality involves setting clear, realistic goals and taking concrete steps towards their attainment, rather than getting lost in vague fantasies or wishful thinking. It also requires discernment and discernment, as we evaluate which desires are truly aligned with our values, purpose, and highest good, and which may lead us astray or distract us from our true path.

Moreover, grounding desire in reality involves cultivating a deep connection to the natural world and the earth's rhythms. Spending time in nature, whether it's tending to a garden, walking in the woods, or just simply sitting outside and observing the world around us, can help to ground us in the present moment and remind us of our interconnectedness with all of creation. By attuning ourselves to the cycles of the seasons, the phases of the moon, and the ebb and flow of life, we can gain a deeper understanding of the impermanence of all things and the inherent wisdom of the natural world. This connection to the earth helps to root our desires in the reality of the here and now, grounding them in the fertile soil of our own being.

Furthermore, grounding desire in reality involves cultivating gratitude and appreciation for the abundance surrounding us. By recognizing and acknowledging the blessings that comes in our lives, we cultivate an attitude of abundance and attract more of what we desire into our experience. Gratitude assist us to shift our priority away from scarcity and lack and towards the infinite possibilities that exist within and around us. When we approach our desires from a place of gratitude, we are more likely to act from a place of abundance rather than fear, making it easier to manifest our intentions and achieve our goals.

In addition to gratitude, grounding desire in reality involves cultivating patience and perseverance in the face of obstacles and setbacks. The path of manifestation is not always linear or straightforward, and we may encounter challenges and delays along the way. Patience allows us to trust in the timing of the universe and surrender to life's flow, knowing that everything unfolds in its perfect time. Perseverance empowers us to stay focused as well as committed to our goals, even when the going gets tough, knowing that every setback is an opportunity for growth and learning. By cultivating patience and perseverance, we demonstrate our commitment to our desires and align ourselves with the natural rhythms of manifestation.

Moreover, grounding desire, in reality, involves aligning our actions with our intentions and taking practical steps toward the realization of our goals. This may involve creating a concrete plan of action, breaking down our goals into manageable tasks, and prioritizing our time and energy accordingly. It may also involve seeking support and guidance from others who can help us along our journey, whether it's through mentorship, collaboration, or simply having someone to hold us accountable. By taking consistent and focused action toward our desires, we demonstrate our commitment and determination to bring them to fruition.

In conclusion, grounding desire in reality is an essential aspect of the alchemical journey, requiring us to anchor our aspirations and intentions in the tangible realm of the physical world. By cultivating a deep connection to the element of Earth, attuning ourselves to the rhythms of nature, and aligning our actions with our intentions, we can manifest our desires and establish the life of our dreams. Grounding desire in reality involves clarity of vision, practicality, and a willingness to do the necessary work to bring our dreams into fruition. Through patience, perseverance, and gratitude, we can navigate the challenges of the manifest world and manifest our deepest desires gracefully and easily.

Air: Cultivating Clarity and Insight

In the alchemical tradition, the element of Air symbolizes intellect, communication, and the realm of thought. It represents the power of the mind to discern truth from falsehood, perceive patterns and connections, and communicate ideas with clarity and precision. Cultivating clarity and insight through the element of Air is an essential aspect of the alchemical journey, enabling practitioners to penetrate the veils of illusion, gain more profound understanding of themselves and the world around them, and align their thoughts, words, and actions with their highest truth.

At its core, cultivating clarity and insight through the element of Air involves quieting the mind's chatter and attuning ourselves to the still, silent space within. This process of inner stillness allows us to access the deeper realms of intuition and wisdom that lie beyond the surface level of thought and perception. Meditation and mindfulness practices serve as powerful tools for cultivating inner stillness, enabling us to observe the movements of our thoughts and emotions with detached awareness, without getting caught up in their endless stream. By cultivating a sense of spaciousness and clarity within the mind, we can gain deeper insight into ourselves and the nature of reality.

Moreover, cultivating clarity and insight through the element of Air involves honing our powers of discernment and critical thinking. In a world inundated with information and distractions, it is essential to develop the ability to discern truth from falsehood, to separate fact from fiction, and to discern the underlying patterns and connections that shape our experience. Critical thinking involves questioning assumptions, examining evidence, and evaluating arguments with logic and reason. By cultivating a skeptical yet open-minded approach to knowledge and experience, we can sharpen our powers of discernment and gain deeper insight into the complexities of the human condition.

Furthermore, cultivating clarity and insight through the element of Air involves developing effective communication skills with ourselves and others. Clear and precise communication is essential for expressing our thoughts, feelings, and intentions with clarity and authenticity, as well as for understanding and empathizing with the perspectives of others. By fostering deeper connections as well as more meaningful relationships, communication skills which include assertiveness, empathy, and active listening help us manage the intricacies of human interaction with ease and grace. We may close the gap between ourselves and others and promote greater understanding and harmony in our relationships by practicing open and honest communication.

In addition to developing effective communication skills, cultivating clarity and insight through the element of Air involves engaging in practices that stimulate the intellect and expand the mind. Reading, studying, and engaging in intellectual discourse help to broaden our horizons, deepen our understanding of the world, and challenge our preconceived notions and beliefs. Exposure to various perspectives and ideas fosters intellectual curiosity and stimulates creative thinking, enabling us to approach problems and difficulties from multiple angles and generate innovative solutions. By developing a lifelong commitment to learning and intellectual inquiry, we can expand our capacity for insight and wisdom and deepen our connection to the element of Air.

Moreover, cultivating clarity and insight through the element of Air involves cultivating a sense of detachment and perspective on our thoughts and emotions. Rather than identifying with our thoughts and emotions as absolute truths, we learn to observe them with detached awareness, recognizing them as transient phenomena that arise and pass away within the space of consciousness. This sense of detachment allows us to gain greater clarity and insight into the nature of our own minds, as well as the conditioned patterns and habits that shape our thoughts and behaviors. By cultivating a sense of detachment, we can free ourselves from the grip of unconscious conditioning and gain greater freedom and autonomy in our lives.

In conclusion, cultivating clarity and insight through the element of Air is an essential aspect of the alchemical journey, enabling practitioners to penetrate the veils of illusion, gain more profound understanding of themselves and the world around them, and align their thoughts, words, and actions with their highest truth. By cultivating inner stillness, honing our powers of discernment and critical thinking, developing effective communication skills, engaging in intellectual inquiry, and cultivating a sense of detachment and perspective on our thoughts and emotions, we can expand our capacity for insight and wisdom and deepen our connection to the element of Air. Through these practices, we can navigate the complexities of the human experience with grace and ease, and align ourselves with the higher principles of truth, beauty, and virtue.

Water: Embracing Emotional Depth

In the alchemical tradition, the element of Water holds a profound significance as the symbol of the emotional realm—the realm of feelings, intuition, and the unconscious. Water represents the fluidity of the human experience, the depth of our emotions, and the power of the unconscious mind to shape our perceptions and behaviors. Embracing emotional depth through the element of Water is an essential aspect of the alchemical journey, enabling practitioners to navigate the depths of the psyche, heal emotional wounds, and cultivate a deeper connection to themselves and others.

At its core, embracing emotional depth involves acknowledging and honoring the full range of human emotions—the joy, the sorrow, the love, the fear, the anger, and everything in between. Rather than suppressing or denying our feelings, we learn to embrace them with compassion and acceptance, recognizing them as messengers that carry essential insights and wisdom from the depths of the unconscious. Through practices such as mindfulness, meditation, and expressive arts, we can create a safe and supportive space for exploring our emotions, allowing them to flow freely and release any pent-up tension or resistance.

Moreover, embracing emotional depth involves developing emotional intelligence—the ability to recognize, understand, as well as manage our own emotions and those of others. Emotional intelligence encompasses skills such as self-awareness, self-regulation, empathy, and social competence, enabling us to navigate human relationships' complexities with grace and authenticity. By cultivating emotional intelligence, we can communicate more effectively, resolve conflicts more constructively, and foster deeper connections with others, leading to greater fulfillment and well-being in our lives.

Furthermore, embracing emotional depth involves exploring the unconscious realms of the psyche, where our deepest fears, desires, and traumas reside. Practices such as dreamwork, journaling, and psychotherapy can help to bring unconscious material into conscious awareness, allowing us to shine the light of awareness on the shadowy corners of our psyche and integrate fragmented aspects of ourselves. By embracing the unconscious, we can heal old wounds, release limiting beliefs, and tap into the deeper wisdom and guidance that lies within us.

In addition to exploring the depths of the unconscious, embracing emotional depth involves cultivating a sense of empathy and compassion for ourselves and others. Empathy is known as the capacity to comprehend and share the feelings of another, while compassion is known as the desire to alleviate the suffering of others. By developing empathy and compassion, we are able deepen our connection to ourselves and others, fostering greater intimacy and understanding in our relationships. Through practices such as loving-kindness meditation and acts of service, we can cultivate a heart that is open and receptive to the joys and sorrows of the world, leading to greater harmony and interconnectedness.

Moreover, embracing emotional depth involves learning to surrender to the flow of emotions, rather than resisting or controlling them. Like the ebb and flow of the tide, emotions come and go in waves, rising and falling in response to the ever-changing currents of life. By surrendering to the flow of emotions, we can learn to ride the waves with grace and ease, trusting in the natural process of emotional healing and transformation. Through practices such as breathwork, body awareness, and somatic experiencing, we can learn to release any stagnant energy or tension held in the body, allowing emotions to flow freely and naturally.

In conclusion, embracing emotional depth through the element of Water is an essential aspect of the alchemical journey, enabling practitioners to navigate the depths of the psyche, heal emotional wounds, and cultivate a deeper connection to themselves and others. By acknowledging and honoring the full range of human emotions, developing emotional intelligence, exploring the unconscious realms of the psyche, cultivating empathy and compassion, and surrendering to the flow of emotions, we can embrace the transformative power of Water and awaken to the depths of our own being. Through these practices, we can heal old wounds, release limiting beliefs, and tap into the deeper wisdom and guidance that lies within us, leading to greater fulfillment, authenticity, and well-being in our lives.

Fire: Igniting Passion and Purpose

In the alchemical tradition, the element of Fire symbolizes the transformative power of passion, creativity, and spiritual illumination. Fire represents the spark of life, the inspiration behind our progress on the path to self-realization and self-discovery. Igniting passion and purpose through the element of Fire is an essential aspect of the alchemical journey, enabling practitioners to tap into their inner fire, unleash their creative potential, and align with their true calling in life.

At its essence, igniting passion and purpose involves tapping into the primal energy of desire—the inner fire that burns within each of us, urging us to pursue our dreams, to fulfill our potential, and follow our passions. This fiery energy fuels our creative impulses, ignites our inspiration, and propels us towards our goals with passion and determination. By developing a profound connection to our inner fire, we can tap into an endless reservoir of energy and vitality, empowering us to overcome obstacles and manifest our dreams with courage and conviction.

Moreover, igniting passion and purpose involves identifying and aligning with our true calling—the unique purpose or mission that gives meaning as well as direction to our lives. Our true calling is often revealed through moments of inspiration, synchronicity, and intuition, guiding us towards activities and pursuits that resonate deeply with our soul. By following our passions and listening to the whispers of our heart, we can uncover our true calling and align our lives with our highest purpose, leading to greater fulfillment, joy, and authenticity.

Furthermore, igniting passion and purpose involves cultivating a mindset of resilience and perseverance in the face of challenges and setbacks. The path of pursuing our passions and fulfilling our purpose is rarely smooth or easy, and we may encounter obstacles, setbacks, and failures along the way. However, it is through facing and overcoming these challenges that we grow stronger, wiser, and more resilient. By cultivating a mindset of resilience, we can learn to embrace challenges as an opportunity for development, and to see setbacks as stepping stones on the path to success.

In addition to cultivating resilience, igniting passion and purpose involves taking inspired action towards our goals and dreams. Inspiration without action is merely a fleeting thought or feeling—it is through taking deliberate and focused action that we bring our dreams into manifestation. By setting clear goals, creating a plan of action, and taking consistent steps towards our vision, we demonstrate our commitment to our passions and purpose, and invite the universe's support in co-creating our reality.

Moreover, igniting passion and purpose involves cultivating a sense of courage and boldness in the pursuit of our dreams. It requires us to step outside of our comfort zones, take risks, as well as embrace the unknown with an open heart and mind. By facing our fears and embracing uncertainty, we expand our comfort zones, tap into our inner strength, and unleash our full creative potential. By pushing past our perceived limitations and embracing our inner fire, we can truly ignite our passion and purpose and create a life of meaning and fulfillment.

In conclusion, igniting passion and purpose through the element of Fire is an essential aspect of the alchemical journey, enabling practitioners to tap into their inner fire, unleash their creative potential, and align with their true calling in life. By developing a more profound connection to our inner fire, identifying and aligning with our true calling, cultivating resilience, taking inspired action, and embracing courage and boldness, we can ignite our passion and purpose and create a life of meaning, fulfillment, and authenticity. Through the transformative power of Fire, we can awaken to our true potential and embark on a journey of self-discovery as well as self-realization that leads to greater joy, fulfillment, and abundance in every area of our lives.

CHAPTER VII

The Alchemist's Laboratory

Creating Sacred Space for Magical Workings

In the practice of magic and mystical arts, creating sacred space is a foundational step in facilitating transformative rituals and workings. Sacred space serves as a container for focusing intention, connecting with higher realms of consciousness, and harnessing the universe's energies to manifest desired outcomes. Whether performing spells, rituals, or ceremonies, creating sacred space is essential for cultivating an environment conducive to spiritual growth, inner transformation, and divine communion.

At its essence, creating sacred space involves setting aside a physical or energetic space dedicated to the practice of magic and spiritual exploration. This space may be a physical location, such as an altar, temple, or meditation room, or it may be an energetic field created through intention and visualization. Regardless of its form, sacred space is imbued with a sense of reverence, sanctity, and intentionality, serving as a portal between the mundane world and the realms of the sacred.

One key element of creating sacred space is purification—the process of cleansing and clearing the space of any negative or stagnant energies that may be present. This may be done through physical means, such as smudging with herbs, lighting candles, or sprinkling blessed water, or it may be done through energetic techniques, such as visualization, intention setting, or energetic clearing rituals. Purification helps to create a clean and clear energetic environment, allowing practitioners to work with greater clarity, focus, and potency.

Moreover, creating sacred space involves consecration—the process of blessing and dedicating the space to a specific purpose or intention. This may involve invoking divine blessings, calling upon spiritual allies or guardians, or performing rituals of dedication and consecration. Consecration imbues the space with a sense of sacredness and purpose, aligning it with the energies of the divine and empowering practitioners to work with greater authority and efficacy.

Another essential element of creating sacred space is intention setting—the conscious and deliberate articulation of the purpose and intention behind the magical working. This may involve clarifying the desired outcome, visualizing the desired end result, and affirming the intention with focused intent and will. Intention setting helps to concentrate the energy and attention of the practitioner, aligning their thoughts, feelings, and actions with the desired outcome and creating a powerful energetic container for manifestation.

Furthermore, creating sacred space involves invoking the elemental energies and spiritual forces that support and guide the magical working. This may involve calling upon the four elements—earth, air, fire, and water—to lend their strength and support to the ritual, as well as invoking specific deities, angels, or spirits that are aligned with the intention of the working. By invoking these elemental and spiritual energies, practitioners can amplify the potency of their magic and create a sacred container for spiritual communion and transformation.

In addition to these elements, creating sacred space may involve using symbolic objects, sacred tools, and ritual gestures to enhance the energetic resonance of the space. This may include placing symbolic objects on the altar, such as crystals, candles, or statues, arranging sacred tools in a specific configuration, such as a pentagram or a circle, or performing ritual gestures, such as tracing symbols or making offerings. These symbolic acts help to externalize and concretize the intention of the working, creating a tangible and potent energetic field that supports the manifestation of desired outcomes.

In conclusion, creating sacred space is essential to magical practice, enabling practitioners to cultivate an environment conducive to spiritual growth, inner transformation, and divine communion. Through purification, consecration, intention setting, invocation, and the use of symbolic objects and gestures, practitioners can create a potent energetic container for magical workings and ritual ceremonies. By honoring the sacredness of space and intention, practitioners are able to tap into the transformative power of magic and make positive change in their lives and in the world around them. Through creating sacred space, practitioners can awaken to the inherent magic and divinity that resides within themselves and all of creation, leading to greater joy, fulfillment, and spiritual awakening.

Tools and Symbols of Alchemy

Alchemy, the ancient mystical tradition, has captivated the imaginations of seekers and scholars for centuries with its enigmatic symbols, arcane rituals, and esoteric teachings. Central to the practice of alchemy are its tools and symbols —objects imbued with deep significance and profound meaning that serve as gateways to the mysteries of the universe. From the philosopher's stone to the alchemical flask, these tools and symbols provide practitioners with a framework for understanding the nature of reality, the process of transformation, and the quest for spiritual enlightenment.

At the heart of alchemy is the quest for the philosopher's stone—the legendary substance said to have the capability to transmute base metals into gold and grant immortality to those who possess it. The philosopher's stone symbolizes the alchemical process of transformation—the journey of inner and outer change, from the leaden aspects of the self to the golden qualities of enlightenment and spiritual awakening. While the philosopher's stone is often depicted as a physical object, it is also understood as a metaphor for realizing one's true nature and attaining spiritual perfection.

Another key alchemy tool is the alchemical flask, also known as the alembic or retort. This vessel serves as a container for the alchemical process, providing a space for transformation. The alchemical flask symbolizes the crucible of consciousness—the vessel of the soul in which the fires of transformation are kindled and the dross of the ego is burned away. Through the process of distillation, sublimation, and fermentation, the alchemical flask facilitates the purification and refinement of the self, allowing practitioners to transmute their base desires into noble aspirations and awaken to their true potential.

In addition to the philosopher's stone and the alchemical flask, alchemy is replete with symbols and imagery that encode profound spiritual truths and esoteric teachings. One of the most famous symbols of alchemy is the ouroboros—the serpent eating its own tail—a symbol of cyclicality, eternity, and the eternal cycle of birth, death, and rebirth. The ouroboros represents the alchemical process of dissolution and reintegration—the breaking down of the old self and the emergence of the new, the death of the ego and the rebirth of the soul.

Another important symbol of alchemy is the alchemical wedding—the union of opposites within the psyche. This symbol represents the integration of masculine and feminine, light and darkness, conscious and unconscious, within the individual. Through the alchemical wedding, practitioners seek to transcend the dualities of the ego and attain a state of wholeness and integration, where all aspects of the self are united in harmony and balance.

Furthermore, alchemy is filled with symbols of the four elements—earth, air, fire, and water—representing creation's building blocks and the universe's fundamental energies. These elements are often depicted as geometric shapes or symbolic images, such as the pentagram, the triangle, the square, and the circle, each of which carries its unique significance and symbolism. By working with the elemental energies, practitioners can tap into the primal forces of creation and harness their power for healing, transformation, and spiritual evolution.

In conclusion, the tools and symbols of alchemy serve as gateways to the mysteries of the universe, providing practitioners with a framework for understanding the nature of reality, the process of transformation, and the quest for spiritual enlightenment. From the philosopher's stone to the alchemical flask, from the ouroboros to the alchemical wedding, these symbols encode profound spiritual truths and esoteric teachings that can transform consciousness and awaken the soul. By working with these tools and symbols, practitioners can unlock the universe's secrets and embark on a journey of self-discovery as well as self-realization that leads to greater joy, fulfillment, and spiritual awakening.

Practical Tips for Effective Magical Practice

Effective magical practice is not merely about casting spells or performing rituals—it is a holistic approach to spiritual growth and self-transformation that requires dedication, discipline, and intentionality. Whether you are a novice practitioner or an experienced magician, some practical tips and strategies can enhance the efficacy of your magical workings and deepen your connection to the universe's mysteries.

One of the most important practical tips for effective magical practice is consistency. Like any skill or discipline, magic requires regular practice and dedication to yield meaningful results. Set aside time each day or week to engage in your magical practice, whether it's meditation, visualization, ritual, or spellwork. Consistency helps build momentum and create a powerful energetic container for your intentions, increasing the likelihood of success in your magical endeavors.

Another practical tip for effective magical practice is mindfulness—the practice of cultivating present moment awareness and focused attention. Before engaging in any magical working, take a few moments to center yourself and ground your energy. Connect with your breath, observe the sensations in your body, and quiet the mind's chatter. By developing mindfulness, you can deepen your connection to the subtle energies of the universe and enhance your ability to work magic with intention and clarity.

In addition to consistency and mindfulness, effective magical practice requires clear intention and focused will. Before performing any magical working, take the time to clarify your intention and articulate your desired outcome with precision and specificity. Visualize the end result as if it has already manifested, and imbue your intention with emotion and conviction. Then, with focused will and determination, direct your energy towards your intention, trusting in the power of your own inner magic to manifest your desires.

Furthermore, effective magical practice involves working with the natural rhythms and cycles of the universe. Pay attention to the moon's phases, the seasons of the year, and the movements of the planets, and time your magical workings accordingly. Certain moon phases are conducive to manifestation, while others are better suited for releasing or letting go. By aligning your magical practice with the cycles of nature, you can amplify the potency of your intentions and work in harmony with the forces of the cosmos.

Moreover, effective magical practice involves working with correspondences—symbols, colors, herbs, and other associations that resonate with your intention and amplify its energy. Research the correspondences associated with your desired outcome, and incorporate them into your magical workings in a meaningful way. For example, if you are performing a love spell, you might use pink candles, rose quartz crystals, and herbs such as rose or jasmine to imporve the energy of love and attraction.

In addition to working with correspondences, effective magical practice entails developing a sense of gratitude and reverence for the magic of everyday life. Take time each day to connect with the natural world's beauty and wonder, and express gratitude for the abundance and blessings in your life. By developing an attitude of gratitude, you can open your heart to the flow of magic and invite more blessings and miracles into your life.

In conclusion, effective magical practice is a multifaceted endeavor that requires dedication, mindfulness, clear intention, and focused will. By cultivating consistency, mindfulness, and clear intention, aligning your practice with the natural rhythms of the universe, working with correspondences, and cultivating gratitude and reverence, you can enhance the efficacy of your magical workings and deepen your connection to the mysteries of the universe. Through regular practice and a willingness to engage with the magic of everyday life, you can awaken to the power of your inner magic and create positive change in your life and the world around you.

CHAPTER VIII

Mastery and Transformation

The Alchemist's Journey: From Novice to Adept

The path of the alchemist is a journey of self-discovery, transformation, and spiritual evolution—a quest for the philosopher's stone and elixir of immortality that leads the practitioner from darkness to light, from ignorance to wisdom, and from leaden existence to golden enlightenment. Like the alchemical process itself, the alchemist's journey unfolds in stages, each building upon the last and leading the practitioner closer to the ultimate goal of self-realization and union with the divine. From novice to adept, the alchemist's journey is one of profound inner alchemy—a journey of awakening to the true nature of reality and the infinite potential that lies within.

At the beginning of the journey, the novice alchemist is like a seed planted in the fertile soil of the psyche, waiting to germinate and grow. The novice is curious, eager, and full of potential, but lacks the knowledge, experience, and discipline necessary to navigate the complexities of the alchemical path. The novice is drawn to the mysteries of the universe, but is easily distracted by the material world's illusions and the ego's temptations. To progress on the journey, the novice must cultivate humility, patience, and a willingness to learn from others who have walked the path before.

As the novice progresses on the journey, they encounter the first stage of alchemical transformation—the nigredo, or blackening. This stage is characterized by darkness, dissolution, and the breaking down of the old self. The novice is confronted with their own shadow—the unconscious aspects of the psyche that have been repressed or denied—and must confront and integrate them to move forward on the path. The nigredo is a period of trial and tribulation, where the novice must face their fears, confront their limitations, and confront the darkness within to emerge into the light of self-awareness and self-acceptance.

Following the nigredo comes the stage of albedo, or whitening. This stage is characterized by purification, illumination, and the emergence of the true self. The novice undergoes a process of inner purification, shedding the layers of conditioning and egoic identification that have obscured their true nature, and uncovering the radiant essence of their being. The albedo is a period of clarity and insight, where the novice gains a deeper understanding of themselves and the world around them, and begins to glimpse the higher truths that lie beyond the veil of illusion.

As the novice progresses further on the journey, they enter the stage of citrinitas, or yellowing. This stage is characterized by integration, synthesis, and the union of opposites. The novice learns to embrace the paradoxes of existence—the light and the dark, the masculine and the feminine, the conscious and the unconscious—and to find harmony and balance within themselves. The citrinitas is a period of alchemical marriage, where the novice unites with their inner divine counterpart and discovers the unity that lies at the heart of all creation.

Finally, the novice reaches the stage of rubedo, or reddening—the culmination of the alchemical journey. This stage is characterized by transmutation, illumination, and the realization of the true self. The novice becomes an adept, a master of their own destiny, and embodies the alchemical maxim "as above, so below; as within, so without." The rubedo is a period of divine union, where the adept merges with the divine and becomes a vessel for the light of consciousness to shine forth into the world.

In conclusion, the alchemist's journey is a profound and transformative process that leads the practitioner from darkness to light, from ignorance to wisdom, and from leaden existence to golden enlightenment. From novice to adept, the alchemist's journey unfolds in stages, each building upon the last and leading the practitioner closer to the ultimate goal of self-realization and union with the divine. Through humility, patience, and a willingness to confront the darkness within, the novice alchemist can progress on the path and awaken to the infinite potential that lies within. Through purification, illumination, and the integration of opposites, the novice can transcend the limitations of the ego and discover the true essence of their being. And through transmutation, illumination, and divine union, the novice can become an adept—a master of their own destiny and a beacon of light in the world.

Overcoming Challenges and Obstacles

In pursuing desire and power, individuals often encounter many challenges and obstacles that test their resolve, resilience, and moral integrity. Desire, with its allure of pleasure and fulfillment, can lead individuals on a quest for personal, social, or spiritual power. However, the journey towards fulfilling desires and harnessing power is rarely straightforward, as it is fraught with internal and external obstacles that must be navigated with care and wisdom.

One of the primary challenges individuals face in pursuing desire and power is the temptation to prioritize personal gain over ethical considerations. The power's allure can be intoxicating, leading individuals to make morally questionable decisions in pursuit of their goals. However, true power lies not in domination or control, but in integrity, authenticity, and compassion. Overcoming this challenge requires individuals to cultivate a strong moral compass, grounded in principles of justice, empathy, and respect for the dignity and autonomy of others.

Moreover, individuals may encounter internal obstacles such as self-doubt, insecurity, or limiting beliefs that undermine their confidence and impede their progress. Pursuing desire and power often requires individuals to step outside their comfort zones, take risks, as well as confront their fears. Overcoming these internal obstacles requires individuals to cultivate self-awareness, practice self-compassion, and challenge negative self-talk. By acknowledging and embracing their vulnerabilities, individuals can tap into their inner strength as well as resilience, allowing them to overcome obstacles and obtain their goals.

In addition to internal obstacles, individuals may also face external challenges such as societal norms, institutional barriers, or systemic injustices that limit their opportunities and hinder their progress. These obstacles may manifest in the form of discrimination, oppression, or marginalization, posing significant barriers to the fulfillment of desires and the attainment of power. Overcoming these external challenges requires individuals to advocate for social change, challenge unjust systems, and work towards creating a more equitable as well as inclusive society. By standing in solidarity with the marginalized communities and also amplifying their voices, individuals can contribute to the collective struggle for justice and equality.

Furthermore, individuals may encounter setbacks and failures along the path toward fulfilling desires and harnessing power. Whether it's a rejection, a setback, or a failure, these experiences can be disheartening and demoralizing. However, setbacks also offer valuable lessons and opportunities for growth. By reframing setbacks as chnaces for learning and resilience-building, individuals can extract wisdom from their experiences and use them to propel them forward. Resilience—known as the ability to bounce back from setbacks and continue moving forward—is essential for overcoming obstacles and achieving success.

In conclusion, overcoming challenges and obstacles in pursuing desire and power requires individuals to cultivate resilience, integrity, and moral courage. Whether facing internal obstacles such as self-doubt and insecurity, or external challenges such as societal norms and institutional barriers, individuals must navigate these obstacles with care and wisdom. Individuals can overcome obstacles and acquire their goals with integrity and authenticity by cultivating self-awareness, practicing self-compassion, and advocating for social change. As they navigate the complexities of desire and power, individuals have the opportunity to fulfill their aspirations and contribute to the greater good, creating a more just, equitable, and compassionate world for all.

Achieving Mastery in Desire and Power

Mastery in desire and power is a journey that requires dedication, discipline, and self-awareness. It is about harnessing the forces of desire and power in service of a higher purpose, cultivating wisdom and integrity along the way. Achieving mastery in desire and power is not about domination or control, but about embodying qualities of authenticity, compassion, and ethical conduct. It demands individuals to navigate the complexities of human desires and power dynamics with integrity and discernment, balancing personal aspirations with a commitment to the greater good.

One key component of achieving mastery in desire and power is self-awareness—the ability to recognize and understand one's own desires, motivations, and impulses.

By cultivating self-awareness, individuals are able to gain insight into the underlying drivers of their behavior, allowing them to make conscious choices and avoid being driven by unconscious impulses. Self-awareness also enables individuals to recognize when their desires are in alignment with their values and when they may be leading them astray, allowing them to course-correct and realign with their true purpose.

Moreover, achieving mastery in desire and power requires individuals to cultivate emotional intelligence—the ability to recognize, understand, and manage their own emotions and those of others. Emotional intelligence enables individuals to navigate intricate social dynamics, establish a strong relationships, and effectively influence others without manipulating or coercion. By developing empathy, compassion, and emotional resilience, individuals can harness the power of emotions in service of their goals while maintaining ethical integrity and authenticity.

In addition to self-awareness and emotional intelligence, achieving mastery in desire and power requires individuals to cultivate resilience—the ability to bounce back from setbacks and adversity. Mastery is not achieved overnight, and individuals are bound to experience difficulties and obstacles along the way. By embracing failure as a chance for growth, learning from setbacks, and being persistent in the face of adversity, individuals can build resilience and develop the tenacity needed to overcome obstacles and achieve their goals.

Furthermore, achieving mastery in desire and power involves cultivating a sense of purpose—a clear vision of what one hopes to achieve and why it matters. Purpose presents individuals with a sense of direction as well as motivation, guiding their actions and decisions in alignment with their values and aspirations. By clarifying their purpose and setting meaningful goals, individuals can harness the power of desire in service of a higher calling, channeling their energy and focus towards realizing their vision.

Moreover, achieving mastery in desire and power requires individuals to cultivate ethical integrity—the commitment to act in alignment with moral principles and values. Mastery is not about amassing power for its own sake but about using power responsibly and ethically to create positive change in the world. By upholding principles of justice, fairness, and compassion, individuals can harness the power of desire in service of the greater good, positively impacting the world around them.

In conclusion, achieving mastery in desire and power is a lifelong journey that demands dedication, self-awareness, and ethical integrity. By cultivating self-awareness, emotional intelligence, resilience, purpose, and ethical integrity, individuals can harness the forces of desire and power in service of a higher purpose, creating positive change in their own lives and in the world around them. Mastery is not about domination or control but about embodying qualities of authenticity, compassion, and ethical conduct, leading to a more just, equitable, and compassionate world for all.

CHAPTER IX

Alchemical Relationships

Romantic and Sexual Alchemy

Romantic and sexual alchemy is a mystical practice that explores the transformative power of love, desire, and intimacy. Rooted in ancient wisdom traditions and esoteric teachings, romantic and sexual alchemy seeks to elevate romantic relationships and sexual experiences to a higher spiritual plane, unlocking the potential for profound healing, growth, and spiritual awakening. At its core, romantic and sexual alchemy is about harnessing the elemental energies of love and desire to transmute base instincts into higher states of consciousness, leading to greater harmony, fulfillment, and union between partners.

Central to romantic and sexual alchemy is the concept of the divine union—the merging of masculine and feminine energies within the individual and in relationship with others. This union symbolizes the alchemical marriage—the integration of opposites within the psyche and the attainment of wholeness and balance. In romantic relationships, the alchemical marriage represents the union of hearts, minds, and souls, creating a sacred space for spiritual growth and mutual evolution. Through the practice of romantic and sexual alchemy, partners can deepen their connection, cultivate intimacy, and unlock the full potential of their relationship.

Moreover, romantic and sexual alchemy involves the cultivation of sacred sexuality—a conscious and intentional approach to sexuality that honors the divine nature of the human body and the sacredness of sexual union. Sacred sexuality is about transcending the purely physical aspects of sex and connecting with the spiritual dimensions of intimacy and pleasure. By engaging in practices such as tantra, mindfulness, and energetic alignment, couples can tap into the transformative power of sexual energy, deepening their connection and expanding their consciousness.

In addition to sacred sexuality, romantic and sexual alchemy also involves exploring archetypal energies and symbols that influence romantic relationships and sexual dynamics. These archetypes, such as the lover, the warrior, the healer, and the magician, represent different aspects of the human psyche and can influence the dynamics of romantic relationships and sexual experiences. By having a knowledge and working with these archetypal energies, couples can gain insight into their relationship dynamics and tap into the deeper layers of meaning and symbolism inherent in their connection.

Furthermore, romantic and sexual alchemy involves the practice of conscious communication and emotional intimacy. Effective communication is necessary for establishing trust, fostering connection, and resolving conflicts in romantic relationships. By cultivating open and honest communication, couples can deepen their understanding of each other, strengthen their bond, and create a secure and supportive space for emotional expression and vulnerability. Emotional intimacy—the ability to connect with and understand the emotions of oneself and one's partner—is essential for building deep and meaningful connections in romantic relationships.

Moreover, romantic and sexual alchemy involves exploring shadow aspects—the unconscious and repressed aspects of the psyche that influence behavior and relationship dynamics. Shadow work is about confronting and integrating these hidden aspects of the self, allowing couples to heal past wounds, release limiting beliefs, and cultivate greater self-awareness and authenticity. By embracing all aspects of themselves and each other, couples can create a more authentic and harmonious relationship based on mutual acceptance, respect, and love.

In conclusion, romantic and sexual alchemy is a profound spiritual practice that explores the transformative power of love, desire, and intimacy. By embracing the principles of divine union, sacred sexuality, archetypal exploration, conscious communication, emotional intimacy, and shadow work, couples can deepen their connection, cultivate greater intimacy, and unlock the full potential of their relationship. Romantic and sexual alchemy is not only about enhancing physical pleasure but about transcending the ego and connecting with the deeper dimensions of the self and the universe. Through the practice of romantic and sexual alchemy, couples can embark on a spiritual growth, healing, and transformation journey, leading to greater harmony, fulfillment, and union in their relationship.

Familial and Social Dynamics in Magical Practice

Magical practice is often perceived as an individual journey, a solitary path of self-discovery and spiritual exploration. However, familial and social dynamics significantly shape and influence one's magical practice, providing a framework for understanding the interconnectedness of personal, familial, and societal energies. Whether inherited through familial traditions or cultivated within social circles, magical practice is deeply intertwined with the dynamics of family relationships, community values, and cultural beliefs.

Within the familial context, magical practice often reflects generational traditions and ancestral wisdom passed down through the ages. Families may have their own rituals, symbols, and practices woven into the fabric of everyday life, shaping each generation's worldview and spiritual beliefs. These familial traditions serve as a source of connection and continuity, fostering a sense of belonging and identity within the family unit. Moreover, familial dynamics can influence the individual's magical practice, as family members may share common beliefs, values, and goals or hold differing perspectives that challenge and expand one's understanding of magic and spirituality.

Furthermore, familial dynamics can impact the transmission of magical knowledge and skills from one generation to the next. In some families, magical practices are openly shared and passed down through formal teachings and initiation rites. In others, magical knowledge may be subtly transmitted through storytelling, folklore, and shared experiences.

Additionally, family dynamics such as parental influence, sibling relationships, and intergenerational conflicts can shape the individual's magical identity and practice, influencing their beliefs, values, and approach to magic.

In addition to familial dynamics, social dynamics also play a crucial role in shaping magical practice. Social circles, spiritual communities, and magical traditions provide a supportive network for individuals to explore and deepen their magical practice. These social dynamics offer opportunities for learning, collaboration, and mutual support, as practitioners come together to share knowledge, experiences, and resources. Moreover, social dynamics can influence the individual's magical identity and practice, as they navigate group dynamics, hierarchies, and power structures within their magical community.

Furthermore, social dynamics can impact the individual's access to magical resources and opportunities for growth. In some communities, magical knowledge and resources may be readily available and accessible, with established institutions, teachers, and mentors offering guidance and support. In others, individuals may face barriers such as discrimination, marginalization, or lack of resources that hinder their ability to engage in magical practice fully. Addressing these social dynamics requires a commitment to creating inclusive and equitable spaces where all individuals can explore and develop their magical potential.

Moreover, social dynamics can influence the individual's magical goals and aspirations, as they navigate their social group's expectations, norms, and values. Peer pressure, social validation, and cultural norms can shape the individual's beliefs, attitudes, and behavior, subtly and profoundly influencing their magical practice. Additionally, social dynamics such as competition, comparison, and conformity can impact the individual's sense of identity and self-worth within their magical community, leading to feelings of insecurity, inadequacy, or imposter syndrome.

In conclusion, familial and social dynamics significantly shape and influence one's magical practice, providing a framework for understanding the interconnectedness of personal, familial, and societal energies. Whether inherited through familial traditions or cultivated within social circles, magical practice is deeply intertwined with the dynamics of family relationships, community values, and cultural beliefs. By acknowledging and embracing these familial and social dynamics, practitioners can cultivate a deeper understanding of themselves and their magical practice, fostering a sense of connection, belonging, and empowerment within their family and community. Through collaboration, mutual support, and collective action, practitioners can work together to develop an inclusive and equitable spaces where all individuals can explore and develop their magical potential, leading to greater harmony, fulfillment, and unity within the magical community and beyond.

Collaborative Magic: Working with Partners and Groups

Traditionally seen as a solitary pursuit, magic can also be a deeply collaborative endeavor. Working with partners and groups allows practitioners to harness collective energies, share knowledge and resources, and amplify the potency of their magical workings. Collaborative magic opens up new possibilities for exploration and growth, fostering deeper connections and fostering a sense of community and shared purpose.

At the heart of collaborative magic is the principle of synergy—the idea that the whole is greater than the sum of its parts. When individuals come together to work magic as a group, they create a powerful energetic field that amplifies the effectiveness of their intentions and rituals. This synergy arises from all participants' combined focus, intention, and energy, leading to greater potency and efficacy in their magical workings.

Moreover, collaborative magic allows practitioners to draw upon diverse skills, perspectives, and experiences, enriching their practice and expanding their understanding of magic. Working with partners and groups provides learning, growth, and mutual support opportunities, as practitioners come together to share knowledge, exchange concepts, and explore new techniques and practices. By collaborating with others, individuals can tap into a collective wisdom that transcends individual limitations, leading to deeper insights and breakthroughs in their magical practice.

Furthermore, collaborative magic fosters a sense of community and shared purpose, creating a supportive network of like-minded individuals who have common goals and values. This sense of belonging and connection can be deeply nourishing and empowering, providing practitioners with a sense of support, validation, and encouragement as they navigate their magical journey. Collaborative magic also offers opportunities for social interaction, friendship, and camaraderie, enriching practitioners' lives and strengthening community bonds.

In addition to the benefits of synergy, learning, and community, collaborative magic also offers practical advantages regarding resource sharing and logistical support. Working with partners and groups allows practitioners to pool their resources, share tools and materials, and divide labor more efficiently, making manifesting their intentions and achieving their goals easier. Moreover, collaborative magic provides a built-in support system, with partners and group members offering feedback, guidance, and assistance as needed, reducing the burden of responsibility on individual practitioners.

However, collaborative magic also comes with its own challenges and considerations. Working with partners and groups requires effective communication, cooperation, and conflict resolution skills to address everyone's needs and concerns. Additionally, practitioners must be mindful of the dynamics of power and hierarchy within their group, ensuring that all members have equal opportunity to contribute and participate in decision-making processes. Collaborative magic also requires a willingness to compromise and adapt, as individuals navigate differing perspectives, preferences, and goals within the group.

In conclusion, collaborative magic offers a powerful and transformative approach to working magic, harnessing partners' and groups' collective energies, knowledge, and resources. By coming together in synergy, practitioners can amplify the potency of their intentions and rituals, deepen their understanding of magic, and foster a sense of community and shared purpose. Collaborative magic provides practical advantages regarding resource sharing and logistical support, while also offering opportunities for learning, growth, and mutual support. However, successful collaboration requires effective communication, cooperation, and conflict-resolution skills as practitioners navigate the dynamics of group interaction and collective decision-making. Ultimately, collaborative magic opens up new possibilities for exploration and growth, enriching the lives of practitioners and strengthening the bonds of community in the magical world and beyond.

CHAPTER X

The Ethical Alchemist

The Impact of Magical Actions on Self and Others

Magical actions, rituals, and intentions hold significant power in shaping the external world and influencing the inner landscape of the individual practitioner and those around them. The impact of magical actions on self and others is profound and multifaceted, with effects that ripple through the fabric of reality, shaping perceptions, experiences, and relationships. Understanding the nature of this impact is essential for responsible and ethical magical practice, as practitioners navigate the complexities of intentionality, responsibility, and accountability in their magical workings.

Magical practice is about harnessing intention and energy to create change by one's will. This process begins with the individual practitioner, whose thoughts, emotions, and desires are the raw material for magical manifestation. Through focused intention, visualization, and ritual, practitioners can channel their energy toward specific goals and outcomes, shaping the trajectory of their lives and experiences. However, the impact of magical actions extends beyond the individual practitioner, influencing the broader collective consciousness and shaping the energetic field of the environment.

Moreover, the impact of magical actions on self and others is not limited to the physical realm but extends into the realms of the psyche, emotions, and spirit. Magical workings can evoke profound shifts in consciousness, triggering insights, revelations, and spiritual awakenings that lead to greater self-awareness and personal growth. Similarly, magical actions can influence emotional states, attitudes, and beliefs, shaping perceptions of self and others and fostering a more profound sense of connection and empathy with the world around them.

Furthermore, the impact of magical actions on others is a significant consideration for practitioners, as they navigate questions of consent, autonomy, and ethical responsibility in their magical workings. While magical intentions may be directed towards specific individuals or groups, practitioners must recognize the inherent complexity and nuance of interpersonal dynamics and respect the free will and sovereignty of others. Coercive or manipulative magic that seeks to override the agency of others is antithetical to the principles of ethical magical practice and can have harmful consequences for both the practitioner and the target of the magic.

In addition to considering the impact of magical actions on others, practitioners must also be mindful of the potential unintended consequences of their workings. The law of cause and effect—often referred to as karma in magical and spiritual traditions—teaches that every action has a corresponding reaction, and that practitioners are responsible for the energetic consequences of their actions. Practitioners must approach their magical workings with humility, integrity, and discernment, recognizing that their actions have far-reaching implications that may extend beyond their immediate intentions.

Furthermore, the impact of magical actions on self and others is influenced by factors such as the practitioner's level of skill and proficiency, the clarity of their intentions, and the alignment of their actions with higher principles and values. Practitioners who approach their magical practice with sincerity, integrity, and a commitment to ethical conduct are more likely to manifest positive outcomes and minimize harm to themselves and others. Conversely, practitioners operating from a place of ego, greed, or selfishness may inadvertently perpetuate negativity and suffering for themselves and those around them.

In conclusion, the impact of magical actions on self and others is profound and far-reaching, with effects that extend beyond the physical realm into the realms of consciousness, emotion, and spirit. Practitioners must approach their magical practice with humility, integrity, and discernment, recognizing the power and responsibility that comes with the practice of magic. By cultivating mindfulness, ethical awareness, and a commitment to the greater good, practitioners can harness the transformative power of magic to create positive change in their lives and in the world around them, fostering greater harmony, balance, and well-being for all.

Karmic Considerations in Alchemical Work

In the practice of alchemy, which seeks to transmute base materials into higher states of being, karmic considerations play a crucial role in understanding the consequences and implications of one's actions. Rooted in the ancient Eastern concept of karma, which posits that every action has a corresponding reaction, karmic considerations in alchemical work emphasize the interconnectedness of all beings and the ethical responsibility of the practitioner to act with integrity, compassion, and wisdom.

At the heart of karmic considerations in alchemical work is the recognition that the energetic patterns and intentions we imbue into our magical workings have far-reaching applications that extend beyond the immediate physical realm. Just as in the practice of traditional alchemy, where the transformation of lead into gold is symbolic of the spiritual journey towards enlightenment, the alchemical practitioner seeks to transmute the base aspects of their being—such as ignorance, greed, and fear—into higher states of consciousness, wisdom, and compassion. However, this process of inner transformation is intimately intertwined with the karmic consequences of one's actions, as practitioners must navigate the law of cause and effect in their quest for spiritual evolution.

Moreover, karmic considerations in alchemical work emphasize the importance of ethical conduct and intentionality in magical practice. The principles of karma remind practitioners that every action, thought, and intention carries an energetic imprint that reverberates throughout the universe, shaping the trajectory of one's life and influencing the experiences of others. Therefore, practitioners must approach their alchemical work with mindfulness, integrity, and a commitment to the greater good, recognizing that their actions have karmic consequences that may extend beyond their immediate awareness.

Furthermore, karmic considerations in alchemical work invite practitioners to cultivate self-awareness and discernment in their magical practice. By examining the motivations, intentions, and energetic patterns underlying their actions, practitioners can gain insight into the karmic implications of their choices and make informed decisions that align with their highest values and aspirations. This process of self-reflection and self-inquiry is integral to the alchemical journey, as practitioners seek to dissolve the illusions of ego and separation and awaken to the interconnectedness of all beings.

In addition to considering the karmic implications of their own actions, practitioners of alchemy must also be mindful of the karmic dynamics inherent in their interactions with others. Just as every individual is subject to the law of karma, so too are relationships, communities, and even entire civilizations. Therefore, practitioners must approach their relationships with integrity, empathy, and compassion, recognizing the interconnectedness of all beings and the impact of their actions on the collective consciousness.

Moreover, karmic considerations in alchemical work highlight the importance of accountability and responsibility in magical practice. Practitioners must take ownership of the energetic consequences of their actions, whether positive or negative, and be willing to learn from their mistakes and shortcomings. This accountability process is essential for growth and evolution, as practitioners seek to align their actions with higher principles and values and contribute to the collective upliftment of humanity.

In conclusion, karmic considerations in alchemical work emphasize the interconnectedness of all beings and the ethical responsibility of the practitioner to act with integrity, compassion, and wisdom. By recognizing the karmic implications of their actions, practitioners can navigate the complexities of magical practice with mindfulness, discernment, and accountability, fostering greater harmony, balance, and well-being for themselves and the world around them. As practitioners engage in the alchemical process of inner transformation, they contribute to the collective evolution of consciousness and the realization of a more enlightened and compassionate society.

Serving the Greater Good: Ethical Responsibility in Magic

Ethical responsibility in magic is a cornerstone of responsible and conscientious practice, emphasizing the importance of using magical powers and abilities for the betterment of oneself, others, and the world at large. Rooted in principles of compassion, integrity, and mindfulness, ethical responsibility in magic guides practitioners in navigating the complexities of magical practice with awareness, discernment, and accountability. At its core, ethical responsibility in magic is about recognizing the interconnectedness of all beings and acting in alignment with higher principles and values that serve the greater good.

The principle of harm none is central to ethical responsibility in magic, which underscores the importance of avoiding actions that cause harm, suffering, or imbalance to oneself, others, or the natural world. This principle, often referred to as the Wiccan Rede or the Law of Threefold Return, reflects the understanding that every action has consequences and that practitioners must be mindful of the impact of their magical workings on the world around them. By approaching magic with compassion and empathy, practitioners can minimize harm and foster greater harmony, balance, and well-being for all beings.

Moreover, ethical responsibility in magic involves honoring the free will and autonomy of others, recognizing that every individual has the right to make their own choices and live their lives according to their own values and beliefs. Practitioners must refrain from coercive or manipulative magic that seeks to override the agency of others, instead fostering environments of consent, respect, and empowerment in their magical workings. By upholding the principles of autonomy and sovereignty, practitioners can cultivate relationships built on trust, integrity, and mutual respect, fostering greater harmony and collaboration in the magical community.

Furthermore, ethical responsibility in magic extends beyond individual actions to encompass the broader impact of magical practice on society and the environment. Practitioners must take into account the ethical implications of their magical workings about social justice, environmental sustainability, and collective well-being, recognizing their role as stewards of the Earth and agents of positive change in the world. By aligning their magical intentions with higher principles and values such as justice, equality, and environmental stewardship, practitioners can contribute to creating a more just, equitable, and sustainable world for all beings.

In addition to considering the ethical implications of their magical actions, practitioners of magic must also be mindful of their intentions, motivations, and energetic patterns underlying their practice. Ethical responsibility in magic involves cultivating self-awareness and discernment in one's magical practice, recognizing the potential for unconscious biases, ego-driven desires, and shadow aspects to influence one's actions and intentions.

By engaging in regular self-reflection and self-inquiry, practitioners can uncover and transform limiting beliefs, fears, and negative thought patterns that may hinder their capacity to act with integrity and compassion.

Moreover, ethical responsibility in magic invites practitioners to engage in ongoing learning and growth, seeking to expand their understanding of ethics, morality, and spirituality in relation to their magical practice. This continuous education and self-improvement process enables practitioners to deepen their ethical awareness, refine their ethical framework, and make educated decisions that align with their highest values and aspirations. By engaging in dialogue with others, seeking out distinct perspectives, and remaining open to feedback and criticism, practitioners can cultivate a more nuanced and holistic understanding of ethical responsibility in magic.

In conclusion, ethical responsibility in magic is a fundamental principle that guides practitioners in navigating the complexities of magical practice with integrity, compassion, and mindfulness. By honoring the principles of harm none, respecting the autonomy of others, and considering the broader impact of their actions on society and the environment, practitioners can contribute to creating a more just, equitable, and sustainable world for all beings. As practitioners serve the greater good through their magical practice, they embody the highest ideals of magic as a transformative force for positive change in the world.

CHAPTER XI

Advanced Techniques and Perspectives

Exploring Sacred Sexuality and Tantra in Magical Practice

Sacred sexuality and tantra have been integral components of magical practice for millennia, offering practitioners profound pathways to spiritual awakening, personal transformation, and union with the divine.

Rooted in ancient spiritual traditions from around the world, sacred sexuality and tantra emphasize the sacredness of the body, the power of sexual energy, and the union of opposites as essential aspects of spiritual growth and enlightenment. By exploring these practices within the context of magical practice, practitioners can tap into the transformative potential of sexual energy to deepen their connection to themselves, their partners, and the divine.

At the heart of sacred sexuality and tantra is the recognition that sexual energy is a potent force for spiritual awakening and personal transformation. In tantra, sexual energy is seen as a divine force that flows through all of creation, animating life and fueling the process of evolution. By harnessing this energy through practices such as breathwork, meditation, and ritualized sex, practitioners can awaken the dormant potentials within themselves, leading to profound states of ecstasy, bliss, and enlightenment. Through cultivating sexual energy, practitioners can tap into the creative power of the universe, allowing them to manifest their intentions with clarity and purpose.

Moreover, sacred sexuality and tantra emphasize the importance of cultivating a deep and intimate connection to oneself and one's partner as essential aspects of spiritual growth and enlightenment. In tantra, the union of opposites—masculine and feminine, light and dark, yin and yang—reflects the divine union of Shiva and Shakti, the cosmic forces of creation and destruction. By embracing the polarities within themselves and their partners, practitioners can transcend the limitations of ego and duality, merging with the divine and experiencing a profound sense of oneness and unity. Through practices such as eye gazing, breathwork, and tantric massage, practitioners can deepen their connection to themselves and their partners, cultivating a sense of intimacy, trust, and communion that transcends the physical realm.

Furthermore, sacred sexuality and tantra offer practitioners powerful tools for healing and transformation on both an individual and collective level. Sexual energy has the power to penetrate the deepest layers of the psyche, releasing old traumas, wounds, and blockages that inhibit personal growth and spiritual evolution. By working with sexual energy consciously and intentionally, practitioners can heal past hurts, resolve inner conflicts, and awaken to their fullest potential as beings of light and love. Moreover, sacred sexuality and tantra offer a pathway to healing and transformation on a collective level, promoting a sense of unity, compassion, as well as empathy that transcends cultural, religious, and societal divisions.

In addition, sacred sexuality and tantra provide practitioners with a framework for integrating spirituality into all aspects of life, which include relationships, work, and daily activities. In tantra, the body is seen as a sacred temple, and all experiences—including eating, sleeping, and working—can be infused with the divine. By cultivating mindfulness, presence, and intentionality in all aspects of life, practitioners can align themselves with the rhythms and cycles of the universe, allowing them to live in harmony with the natural world and manifest their intentions with grace and ease.

Moreover, sacred sexuality and tantra offer practitioners a pathway to union with the divine—the ultimate goal of spiritual practice. In tantra, the union of Shiva and Shakti represents the merging of the individual soul with the cosmic consciousness, leading to a state of divine ecstasy and bliss. By cultivating a deep and intimate connection to oneself, one's partner, and the divine, practitioners can transcend the limitations of the ego and encounter a profound sense of oneness and unity with all of creation. Through practices such as meditation, prayer, and ritualized sex, practitioners can merge with the divine and awaken to their true nature as beings of light and love.

In conclusion, sacred sexuality and tantra offer practitioners profound pathways to spiritual awakening, personal transformation, and union with the divine. By exploring these practices within the context of magical practice, practitioners can tap into the transformative potential of sexual energy to deepen their connection to themselves, their partners, and the divine. Whether through practices such as breathwork, meditation, or ritualized sex, sacred sexuality and tantra provide practitioners with powerful tools for healing, growth, and enlightenment on both an individual and collective level. Thus, by embracing the principles of sacred sexuality and tantra in their magical practice, practitioners can unlock the deepest universe's mysteries and awaken to their true nature as beings of light and love.

Working with Archetypes and Symbols to Amplify Desire Magic

In the realm of magic, archetypes and symbols serve as potent tools for amplifying the power of desire and manifesting intentions into reality. Archetypes are universal patterns or themes that reside within the collective unconscious, representing fundamental aspects of the human experience such as love, power, wisdom, and transformation. Symbols, on the other hand, are visual or auditory representations of these archetypal themes, imbued with deep meaning and significance. By working with archetypes and symbols in their magical practice, practitioners can tap into the collective wisdom of the unconscious mind, accessing vast reservoirs of energy and insight to amplify their desires and manifest their intentions with clarity and purpose.

One of the key ways in which practitioners can work with archetypes and symbols to amplify desire magic is through visualization and meditation. By visualizing themselves embodying the qualities and attributes of a specific archetype—such as the lover, the warrior, or the magician—practitioners can tap into the archetypal energies that resonate with their desires, amplifying their intentions and increasing their likelihood of manifestation. Similarly, by meditating on symbols that represent their desires—such as hearts for love, swords for power, or keys for unlocking hidden potentials—practitioners can imbue these symbols with energy and intention, allowing them to act as powerful conduits for manifestation.

Moreover, practitioners can work with archetypes and symbols in their magical rituals and spells to amplify the energy and intention behind their workings. For example, a practitioner seeking to manifest love in their life may incorporate symbols such as roses, hearts, and Cupid into their rituals, invoking the energy of the lover archetype to amplify their desires. Similarly, a practitioner seeking to manifest abundance and prosperity may work with symbols such as coins, keys, and the god Hermes, invoking the energy of the merchant archetype to increase their wealth and success. By aligning their rituals with archetypal energies and symbols that resonate with their desires, practitioners can amplify the power of their magic and manifest their intentions with greater ease and effectiveness.

Furthermore, practitioners can work with archetypes and symbols in their magical journaling and dreamwork to gain insights into their desires and intentions. Journaling allows practitioners to explore their thoughts, feelings, and desires in a safe and supportive space, helping them to uncover hidden truths and insights that may be blocking their manifestation. By writing about their desires and intentions in relation to specific archetypes and symbols, practitioners can gain clarity and perspective on their goals, allowing them to align their actions with their highest aspirations. Similarly, practitioners can work with archetypal symbols in their dreams, interpreting the messages and guidance that arise from the unconscious mind to deepen their understanding of their desires and intentions.

In addition, practitioners can work with archetypes and symbols in their everyday lives to create talismans, amulets, and other magical objects that serve as powerful conduits for manifestation. By imbuing these objects with the energy and intention of a specific archetype or symbol, practitioners can carry the essence of their desires with them wherever they go, aligning themselves with the energies of the universe and increasing their likelihood of manifestation. For example, a practitioner seeking to manifest protection and safety may create a talisman in the shape of a shield, invoking the energy of the warrior archetype to ward off harm and negativity. Similarly, a practitioner seeking to manifest creativity and inspiration may create a talisman in the shape of a paintbrush, invoking the energy of the artist archetype to unlock their creative potential and bring their visions to life.

In conclusion, working with archetypes and symbols is a powerful way to amplify desire magic and manifest intentions into reality. By tapping into the collective wisdom of the unconscious mind, practitioners can access vast reservoirs of energy and insight to amplify their desires and increase their likelihood of manifestation. Whether through visualization and meditation, ritual and spellwork, journaling and dreamwork, or the creation of magical objects, practitioners can work with archetypes and symbols in different ways to deepen their understanding of their desires and intentions, aligning themselves with the energies of the universe and unlocking their fullest potential as magical beings. Thus, by embracing the power of archetypes and symbols in their magical practice, practitioners can amplify their desire magic and manifest their intentions with clarity, purpose, and effectiveness.

Incorporating Elemental and Planetary Energies in Desire-Alchemy

In the practice of desire-alchemy, practitioners harness the elemental and planetary energies of the universe to amplify their intentions and manifest their desires with precision and effectiveness. Rooted in ancient mystical traditions and esoteric wisdom, understanding elemental and planetary energies provides practitioners with a powerful framework for understanding the forces at work in the world and aligning themselves with the rhythms and cycles of nature. By incorporating these energies into their desire-alchemy practice, practitioners can tap into the elemental and planetary currents that govern the universe, harnessing their power to catalyze profound transformation and manifestation.

The elements—earth, air, fire, and water—are fundamental building blocks of the physical world, each possessing its own unique qualities, attributes, and correspondences. Earth represents stability, grounding, and manifestation, while air embodies intellect, communication, and inspiration. Fire symbolizes passion, creativity, and transformation, while water signifies emotion, intuition, and flow. By working with the elemental energies in their desire-alchemy practice, practitioners can tap into the inherent qualities of each element to amplify their intentions and manifest their desires with greater clarity and purpose. For example, a practitioner seeking to manifest abundance and prosperity may work with the earth element, invoking its stability and grounding qualities to anchor their intentions in the physical realm. Similarly, a practitioner seeking to manifest inspiration and creativity may work with the element of air, harnessing its intellectual and communicative energies to channel their ideas and insights into tangible form.

In addition to the elements, practitioners also work with the energies of the planets to enhance their desire-alchemy practice. Each planet is interconnected with specific qualities, attributes, and correspondences that influence different aspects of human experience and consciousness. For example, the sun represents vitality, leadership, and self-expression, while the moon symbolizes intuition, emotion, and cycles of change. By working with planetary energies in their desire-alchemy practice, practitioners can tap into the celestial currents that govern the universe, aligning themselves with the cosmic forces that influence their intentions and desires. For example, a practitioner seeking to manifest success and recognition in their career may work with the sun's energy, invoking its power and vitality to propel them towards their goals. Similarly, a practitioner seeking to manifest emotional healing and transformation may work with the energy of the moon, harnessing its intuitive and nurturing energies to support their inner journey.

Moreover, practitioners can incorporate elemental and planetary correspondences into their desire-alchemy rituals and spells to amplify the energy and intention behind their workings. For example, a practitioner seeking to manifest love and romance may create a ritual altar adorned with symbols and objects representing the element of water—such as seashells, crystals, and images of the ocean—to invoke the emotional and intuitive energies needed to attract a soulmate. Similarly, a practitioner seeking to manifest abundance and prosperity may perform a ritual during a planetary hour ruled by Jupiter, the planet of expansion and growth, to amplify their intentions and increase their likelihood of success. By aligning their rituals with elemental and planetary energies that resonate with their desires, practitioners can amplify the power of their desire-alchemy practice and manifest their intentions with greater ease and effectiveness.

Furthermore, practitioners can work with the elemental and planetary energies in their daily lives to support their desire-alchemy practice and align themselves with the rhythms and cycles of nature. For example, a practitioner seeking to cultivate a deeper connection to the earth element may spend time outdoors gardening, hiking, or simply sitting in nature, grounding themselves in the physical world and attuning themselves to the energies of the earth. Similarly, a practitioner seeking to align themselves with the energy of a specific planet may perform daily rituals or meditations during the planetary hour associated with that planet, allowing them to tap into its unique qualities and correspondences and amplify their desire-alchemy practice.

In conclusion, incorporating elemental and planetary energies into desire-alchemy practice provides practitioners with a powerful framework for amplifying their intentions and manifesting their desires with precision and effectiveness. By working with the elemental energies of earth, air, fire, and water, practitioners can tap into the inherent qualities of each element to anchor their intentions in the physical realm, channel their ideas and insights into tangible form, and flow with the natural rhythms as well as cycles of life. Similarly, by working with the planets' energies, practitioners can align themselves with the cosmic forces that govern the universe, harnessing their power to propel them towards their goals and desires. Thus, by incorporating elemental and planetary energies into their desire-alchemy practice, practitioners can amplify the power of their magic and manifest their intentions with clarity, purpose, and effectiveness.

Pushing Boundaries: Exploring the Outer Edges of Desire Magic

In the realm of magic, desire is a potent force that drives transformation, manifestation, and personal evolution. It is the fuel that propels practitioners forward on their spiritual journey, empowering them to manifest their deepest longings and wildest dreams into reality. Yet, within the practice of desire magic exists a realm beyond the familiar boundaries of convention and expectation—a realm where practitioners dare to explore the outer edges of their desires, pushing beyond the limits of what is considered possible or acceptable. Within this uncharted territory, practitioners can tap into the full potential of desire magic, unlocking hidden depths of power, creativity, and transformation that lie dormant within themselves.

At the heart of pushing boundaries in desire magic lies the willingness to challenge societal norms, cultural conditioning, and personal limitations to pursue one's deepest desires. It requires practitioners to question the status quo, to defy conventional wisdom, and to embrace the unknown with courage and conviction. By pushing beyond the boundaries of what is considered acceptable or possible, practitioners open themselves up to new possibilities, new perspectives, and new ways of being in the world. They embrace the role of the rebel, the renegade, and the revolutionary—unafraid to challenge the prevailing order and forge their own path toward personal and spiritual liberation.

One way in which practitioners push boundaries in desire magic is by exploring taboo or forbidden desires—those aspects of themselves that society deems unacceptable or inappropriate. These desires may be rooted in primal instincts, suppressed emotions, or repressed aspects of the psyche, and they often carry a potent charge of energy that can be harnessed for transformation as well as manifestation. By confronting these taboo desires head-on, practitioners can reclaim their power, liberate themselves from shame and guilt, and tap into the raw, primal energy that lies at the core of their being. They embrace the shadow—the dark, mysterious, and often misunderstood aspects of themselves—and integrate it into their practice, harnessing its power to fuel their desires and propel them towards their goals.

Moreover, practitioners push boundaries in desire magic by exploring the outer reaches of their imagination, daring to dream bigger, bolder, and more audaciously than ever before. They transcend the limitations of the rational mind, tapping into the boundless creativity and limitless potential of the subconscious to envision realities that defy logic and reason. They embrace the role of the visionary, the dreamer, the architect of worlds—allowing their imaginations to run wild and their fantasies to take flight. By pushing the boundaries of their imagination, practitioners open themselves up to new realms of possibility, new dimensions of reality, and new avenues for manifestation. They dare to dream the impossible dream, and in doing so, they unlock the power to make it a reality.

Furthermore, practitioners push boundaries in desire magic by experimenting with unconventional or innovative techniques and practices. They seek out new methods, new modalities, and new approaches to manifestation, unbound by tradition or precedent. They embrace the role of the pioneer, the explorer, the trailblazer—forging new paths and breaking new ground in pursuing their desires. Whether through experimental rituals, cutting-edge technology, or avant-garde artistic expression, practitioners push the boundaries of what is considered possible or acceptable, opening up new vistas of possibility and potential. They refuse to be bound by convention or conformity; instead, they embrace the freedom to explore, experiment, and evolve in their practice.

Moreover, practitioners push boundaries in desire magic by engaging in acts of radical self-expression and self-empowerment. They embrace their individuality, authenticity, and sovereignty, refusing to conform to societal expectations or external pressures. They reclaim their power, their autonomy, and their agency—asserting their right to define their desires, their own identities, and their destinies. By pushing the boundaries of self-expression, practitioners liberate themselves from the constraints of fear, shame, and self-doubt, allowing their true selves to shine forth in all their brilliance and beauty. They become the architects of their reality, the masters of their destiny, and the creators of their magic.

In conclusion, pushing boundaries in desire magic is a bold and audacious act of self-liberation and self-empowerment. It requires practitioners to challenge the status quo, defy conventional wisdom, and embrace the unknown with courage and conviction. By exploring taboo desires, expanding the boundaries of imagination, experimenting with innovative techniques, and engaging in radical self-expression, practitioners tap into the full potential of desire magic, unlocking hidden depths of power, creativity, and transformation that lie dormant within themselves. They become the pioneers, the visionaries, the architects of their destiny—forging new paths, breaking new ground, and manifesting their wildest dreams into reality. Thus, by pushing the boundaries of desire magic, practitioners embrace the limitless potential of their being, unlocking the power to create the life they truly desire and deserve.

CHAPTER XII

Integration and Reflection

Synthesizing Desire, Power, and Magic

Synthesizing desire, power, and magic is a profound endeavor that lies at the intersection of personal growth, spiritual evolution, and mystical exploration. Desire, power, and magic are intrinsic aspects of the human experience, each holding the potential for both liberation and limitation, depending on how they are understood, harnessed, and integrated into one's life. At their core, desire and power are primal forces that drive human behavior and shape the course of individual and collective destiny. On the other hand, magic is the art and science of harnessing these forces to create change according to one's will. Synthesizing desire, power, and magic involves cultivating a deeper understanding of these forces, embracing their transformative potential, and using them to awaken to higher states of consciousness and being.

Desire, often portrayed as a force to be transcended or overcome in spiritual traditions, is an essential aspect of the human experience that drives growth, creativity, and evolution. It is the fuel that propels individuals toward their goals, aspirations, and dreams, motivating them to strive for excellence and fulfillment in all areas of life. However, desire can also become a source of suffering and attachment when it is rooted in ego, craving, and aversion. Synthesizing desire in the context of magic involves cultivating a balanced relationship with one's desires, recognizing their inherent impermanence and the importance of aligning them with higher principles and values. By harnessing the power of desire with mindfulness and discernment, practitioners can channel their energy towards noble goals and aspirations that serve the greater good.

Power, often associated with control, domination, and manipulation, is another intrinsic aspect of the human experience that shapes relationships, institutions, and societies. However, power is not inherently good or evil but instead a neutral force that can be utilized for positive or negative ends, depending on the intentions and values of the wielder. Synthesizing power in the context of magic involves recognizing one's personal power and agency, as well as the ethical responsibilities that come with it. It is about cultivating power with humility, integrity, and compassion, using it to empower oneself and others, and create positive change in the world. By harnessing the power of intentionality and focused attention, practitioners can manifest their desires and intentions with greater clarity, precision, and effectiveness.

Magic, the art and science of harnessing the unseen forces of the universe to make change, is the bridge that connects desire and power, allowing practitioners to manifest their intentions and transform reality according to their will. Synthesizing magic involves mastering the principles and techniques of magical practice, such as visualization, ritual, meditation, and energy work, to channel the energies of desire and power towards specific goals and outcomes. It is about cultivating a deep relationship with the unseen realms of existence, tapping into the wisdom of the ancestors, spirits, and archetypes, and aligning oneself with the natural rhythms and cycles of the universe. By honing their magical skills and developing a more profound understanding of the interconnectedness of all things, practitioners can co-create with the universe and become agents of positive change in their own lives and in the world.

Furthermore, synthesizing desire, power, and magic involves integrating these forces into a coherent, harmonious whole that reflects the practitioner's highest aspirations and values. It is about aligning one's desires with the greater good, using power responsibly and ethically, and practicing magic with integrity and mindfulness. This synthesis process requires self-awareness, self-discipline, and a willingness to confront and transform the shadow aspects of the self that may hinder one's spiritual evolution and magical practice. By embracing the transformative potential of desire, power, and magic, practitioners can awaken to higher states of consciousness and being, and contribute to the co-creation of a more just, equitable, and compassionate world for all beings.

In conclusion, synthesizing desire, power, and magic is a profound and transformative journey that requires courage, commitment, and self-awareness. It is about recognizing the inherent power and potential of one's desires, cultivating personal power with humility and integrity, and harnessing the forces of magic to create positive change in the world. By embracing the transformative potential of desire, power, and magic, practitioners can awaken to their highest potential and become agents of healing, transformation, and liberation in their own lives and in the world.

Personal Reflections on the Alchemical Journey

The alchemical journey is a profound and transformative process of inner exploration, spiritual evolution, and self-discovery. Rooted in ancient wisdom and mystical traditions, the alchemical journey is a symbolic and metaphorical quest for personal and spiritual enlightenment, wherein the practitioner seeks to transmute the base aspects of their being into higher states of consciousness and being. Throughout history, alchemy has been regarded as both a literal and metaphorical practice, with practitioners striving to uncover the secrets of the universe and unlock the mysteries of existence. However, at its core, the alchemical journey is a deeply personal and subjective experience, unique to each individual practitioner.

One of the central themes of the alchemical journey is transformation—the idea that through inner work, self-reflection, and spiritual practice, individuals can undergo profound shifts in consciousness and identity. This process of transformation is often depicted symbolically as base metals' transmutation into gold, symbolizing the journey from ignorance and limitation to enlightenment and liberation. However, the alchemical journey is not limited to physical or material transformation but encompasses the full spectrum of human experience, including psychological, emotional, and spiritual growth.

Moreover, the alchemical journey is a journey of integration—of bringing together the disparate elements of the self into a coherent and harmonious whole. This integration process involves confronting and reconciling the shadow aspects of the self—the unconscious fears, traumas, and unresolved issues that hinder one's spiritual evolution. By embracing the shadow and integrating its lessons, practitioners can reclaim lost parts of themselves and awaken to their true nature as divine beings of light and love.

Furthermore, the alchemical journey is a journey of alchemical marriage—a symbolic union of opposites, such as masculine and feminine, light and dark, conscious and unconscious. This process of integration and reconciliation involves embracing the polarities of existence and finding balance and harmony within oneself. By uniting the disparate aspects of the self, practitioners can transcend duality and experience a state of wholeness and unity with the cosmos.

In addition, the alchemical journey is a journey of spiritual awakening—a process of remembering and reconnecting with the divine essence that resides within each individual. This awakening process involves peeling back the layers of conditioning and illusion that obscure one's true nature and recognizing the inherent divinity that lies at the core of the self. By cultivating practices such as meditation, prayer, and contemplation, practitioners can attune themselves to the higher realms of consciousness and align with the divine will.

Moreover, the alchemical journey is a journey of service—a commitment to using one's newfound wisdom and insight for the betterment of oneself, others, and the world at large. This service process involves embodying the principles of love, compassion, and altruism in all aspects of one's life and using one's gifts and talents to contribute to the greater good. By sharing the fruits of their spiritual labor with others, practitioners can inspire and uplift those around them and help co-create a more just, equitable, and compassionate world for all beings.

In conclusion, the alchemical journey is a profound and transformative process of inner exploration, spiritual evolution, and self-discovery. Rooted in ancient wisdom and mystical traditions, the alchemical journey invites practitioners to embark on a quest for personal and spiritual enlightenment, wherein they seek to transmute the base aspects of their being into higher states of consciousness and being. Through transformation, integration, and spiritual awakening, practitioners can awaken to their true nature as divine beings of light and love and contribute to co-creating a more just, equitable, and compassionate world for all beings.

Continuing the Path: Lifelong Learning and Growth

The journey of personal and spiritual development is a lifelong endeavor that unfolds through a process of continuous learning, growth, and self-discovery. Rooted in the principles of curiosity, openness, and humility, continuing the path of personal and spiritual growth involves an ongoing commitment to deepening one's understanding of oneself, the world, and the mysteries of existence. Whether through formal education, spiritual practice, or life experience, the path of lifelong learning offers infinite opportunities for exploration, expansion, and transformation, inviting individuals to embrace the journey with courage, curiosity, and a sense of wonder.

Central to continuing the path of lifelong learning is the recognition that growth and evolution are inherent aspects of the human experience. Just as the natural world undergoes cycles of birth, growth, death, and rebirth, so do individuals experience periods of growth, stagnation, and renewal. By embracing the cyclical nature of existence and remaining open to the lessons and opportunities that arise, individuals can navigate the ups and downs of life with grace, resilience, and a sense of purpose.

Moreover, continuing the path of lifelong learning involves cultivating a growth mindset—a belief in one's ability to learn, adapt, as well as grow in response to challenges and setbacks. Rather than viewing obstacles as insurmountable barriers, individuals that have a growth mindset view them as chances for learning, growth, and self-improvement. By cultivating a resilience, perseverance, and optimism mindset, individuals can overpower difficulties as well as thrive in the face of uncertainty, realizing their full potential and manifesting their deepest aspirations.

Furthermore, continuing the path of lifelong learning requires a commitment to self-reflection and self-inquiry, as individuals seek to deepen their understanding of themselves, their beliefs, and their motivations. Through meditation, journaling, and introspection, individuals can explore the depths of their inner landscape, uncover hidden truths, and illuminate blind spots that may hinder their growth and evolution. By cultivating self-awareness and self-compassion, individuals can embrace the full spectrum of their humanity and cultivate greater authenticity, resilience, and well-being.

In addition, continuing the path of lifelong learning involves a willingness to explore new ideas, perspectives, and ways of being that may challenge one's existing beliefs and assumptions. By remaining open-minded and receptive to the wisdom of others, individuals can expand their horizons, broaden their understanding of the world, and cultivate empathy and compassion for those with different experiences and viewpoints. Through dialogue, collaboration, and engagement with diverse perspectives, individuals can deepen their understanding of themselves as well as the world, fostering greater harmony, understanding, and connection with others.

Moreover, continuing the path of lifelong learning involves a commitment to personal and spiritual development, as individuals seek to align their actions and intentions with higher principles and values. Whether through formal study, spiritual practice, or service to others, individuals can deepen their connection to the divine and cultivate qualities such as love, compassion, and wisdom that are essential for personal and collective well-being. By living with integrity, authenticity, and purpose, individuals can inspire as well as uplift those around them, contributing to the co-creation of a more just, equitable, and compassionate world for all beings.

In conclusion, continuing the path of lifelong learning is a sacred journey of self-discovery, growth, and transformation that unfolds through a commitment to curiosity, openness, and humility. By embracing the cyclical nature of existence, cultivating a growth mindset, and engaging in self-reflection and self-inquiry, individuals can navigate life's challenges with grace, resilience, and a sense of purpose. Through dialogue, collaboration, and engagement with diverse perspectives, individuals can deepen their understanding of themselves as well as the world, fostering greater harmony, understanding, and connection with others. Ultimately, continuing the path of lifelong learning is a journey of personal and spiritual evolution that invites individuals to embrace the fullness of their humanity and contribute to the co-creation of a more just, equitable, and compassionate world for all beings.

CONCLUSION

In "The Alchemy of Desire: Fusing Passion with Power in Magical Practice," readers have embarked on a profound exploration of the intersection between desire, power, and magic, uncovering the transformative potential inherent in the synthesis of these elements. Throughout the pages of this book, we have delved into the depths of the human psyche, the mysteries of the universe, and the intricate interplay between personal growth, spiritual evolution, and mystical practice.

At the heart of this exploration lies the recognition that desire, power, and magic are not isolated phenomena but interconnected aspects of the human experience, each holding the key to unlocking hidden potentials and awakening to higher states of consciousness and being. Through the lens of alchemical symbolism, readers have gained insight into the transformative power of desire's fire, the ethical responsibilities of wielding power, and the profound mysteries of magical practice.

Moreover, this book has served as a guide for practitioners on personal and spiritual development, offering practical insights, philosophical reflections, and mystical wisdom to support them in their journey. From historical and cultural perspectives on desire to psychological insights into its workings, from the alchemical symbolism of desire's fire to the ethical considerations of power dynamics, readers have been equipped with a comprehensive understanding of the forces at play in their magical practice. Furthermore,

"The Alchemy of Desire" has emphasized the importance of ethical responsibility, mindfulness, and integrity in magical practice, reminding practitioners of the interconnectedness of all beings and the impact of their actions on the world around them. Through rituals, spells, meditations, and visualizations, readers have been invited to harness the transformative power of desire and power for the greater good, fostering harmony, balance, and well-being in their lives and in the world.

As readers conclude this book, they are reminded that the journey of alchemy is not merely an intellectual exercise but a lived experience—a journey of self-discovery, growth, and transformation that unfolds through a commitment to lifelong learning and growth. By continuing to cultivate a growth mindset, engage in self-reflection and self-inquiry, and align their actions and intentions with higher principles and values, readers can deepen their understanding of themselves and the world, contribute to the co-creation of a more just, equitable, and compassionate world, and realize their fullest potential as alchemists of the soul.

In essence, "The Alchemy of Desire: Fusing Passion with Power in Magical Practice" serves as a roadmap for the journey of personal and spiritual evolution, guiding readers on a transformative path of self-discovery, growth, and empowerment. Through its pages, readers have gained insight into the mysteries of desire, power, and magic, and have been empowered to harness these forces for positive change in their lives and in the world. As they continue on their journey, may they carry with them the wisdom, insights, and inspiration gleaned from this book, and may they continue to shine their light brightly as agents of transformation and healing in the world.